CW00402703

# SEA POEMS

A Seafarer Anthology

*To friends and family,*
*the latter of whom have voyaged out*
*all over the world*

# SEA POEMS

## A Seafarer Anthology

Selected and introduced by

## BOB CREW

SEAFARER BOOKS
SHERIDAN HOUSE

Published 2005 by

Seafarer Books · 102 Redwald Road · Rendlesham · Suffolk IP12 2TE · England

and

Sheridan House Inc · 145 Palisade Street · Dobbs Ferry · NY 10522 · USA

UK ISBN 0 9547062 6 9 · USA ISBN 1 57409 214 6

British Library Cataloging-in-Publication Data

Sea poems : a seafarer anthology
1. Sea poetry, English
2. Sea poetry, American
I. Crew, Bob
821'.008032162

ISBN-10: 0954706269

Library of Congress Cataloging-in-Publication Data

Sea poems: a seafarer anthology / selected and introduced by Bob Crew.
p. cm.
ISBN 1-57409-214-6 (alk. paper)
1. Sea poetry, American. 2. Seafaring life — Poetry.
3. Atlantic Ocean—Poetry. 4. Sea poetry, English. I. Crew, Bob.

PS595.S39S43 2005
811.008'032162—dc22

2005016895

Text set digitally in Proforma
Typesetting and design by Louis Mackay
Printed by Cromwell Press · Trowbridge · England

# Contents

# Preface

T his hands-across-the-sea anthology of British and American poetry does not include every sea poem ever published in the English language. It is, rather, a personal collection of some of my favourite poems from both sides of the Atlantic, and for this reason there are other poems left out, either because they do not happen to be my favourites, or because of space restrictions in a book of this size. Some well-known poems have been excluded because they seem to me to be too hackneyed or boring. On the other hand, there are others that are included that are not particularly well known, but which are favourites of mine, and there is no shortage of popular sea poems that are everybody's favourites.

The inclusion of a goodly number of my own poems is by invitation of the publisher, and in most cases I have written poems to fill in the gaps that exist in the history of English-language sea poetry – with regard to particular events or aspects of seafaring that are not covered by other poets – and I have done this in order to achieve a fuller picture and to update this collection. Quite a number of the most famous English poets, past and present, have not written a great volume of poetry about the sea – they have been busy writing about other things besides – which is why there are perhaps only one or two of their poems included. The exception is John Masefield, a seafarer who wrote a great deal about the sea, and he is well represented, given his own showpiece section, because his poems strike me as being in a class of their own. There is also a stand-alone *Battle of Trafalgar* section, since this book is published in the year of its bicentenary.

This is a very different kind of anthology from others, because it is primarily for seafarers, and it brings together two separate nations and cultures that have shared the same maritime convictions, concerns, ideas and experiences whilst also sharing – or being divided by! – the same language. This is also an anthology that analyses and interprets the poetry on offer, and it includes newly grown poems of its own that are specifically written for it, with a view to giving it a freshness and shape all its own. Whilst old poems have been taken from dusty library shelves, new ones have been added to the mix in order to complement and/or respond to what has gone before, as well as to respond to the ongoing call of the sea. Whilst this may be considered a good or a bad thing, this is a work that is doing something completely different with the time-honoured convention of poetry anthologies, as it breaks new ground, and this may be of literary or academic interest.

Whilst I have provided some biographical details of American poets for the majority of my (British) readers – many of whom will be unfamiliar with American poets – I have not done this with British poets and this is because they are too numerous and will probably need no introduction in Britain. There are too many British poets for their biographical details to be included within the pages of what is not exactly an enormous volume of verse, while there are only five American poets in these pages (but with a considerable volume of poetry to their credit). I have made an exception of John Masefield amongst the British poets because, as I say, I regard him as a special case, of particular biographical interest to seafarers on both sides of the Atlantic.

In making my choice of poems, I have gone for the most radiant, graphic, imagist, rousing and spiritually uplifting works, but there are some informational, gritty and 'reality' poems included also. There is blank verse, free verse and rhyming poetry in these pages, and I have included poems that give a strong historical sense of Britain's seafaring heritage and of London as the centre of the world, as well as a sense of the special relationship that has developed with the United States of America. I have furthermore gone for poems that demonstrate how seafaring has influenced the way that poets think, and how the maritime atmosphere to which seafaring has given rise has influenced the thoughts of poets on land when writing, not only about the sea, but also about other matters, in which they have used sea imagery. Seafaring has had a big influence on English language usage, of course, as is clear from the great many words, sayings and phrases that we take from the sea, and it has had a

big influence on our poetry likewise. Our language and prose –
and not just poetry – is awash with sea imagery and terminology.

There are in these pages soulful and gentle poems, rough and
ready poems, wild and adventurous poems – some that voyage
out and others that voyage in or somewhere in between.
For this reason – with the exception of the American poets, who
are grouped together – I have themed the British poems under
voyaging headings – out, in, and in between.

There are two former officers of the British Merchant Navy –
friends of mine – to whom thanks are owed.

Special thanks are due to Tony Wardle of Bullyhole Bottom
in Monmouthshire (near Chepstow) – who was an officer in the
Merchant Navy with Elder Dempster – because he first got me
interested in the sea with so many ripping yarns about it, and he
has usefully explained some technical matters and terminologies
while I have been compiling this anthology and writing
commentaries and poems for it.

Thanks are also due to Ian Craig, of Sevenoaks in Kent, a
former Merchant Navy officer with P&O, who has told me all
about dirty British coasters, whilst also taking the trouble to
explain certain oddities of the British merchant fleet.
I am grateful to them both for their time.

Bob Crew
*London*
*April 2005*

## READING THE SEA

Seafarers read the sea like other people read books.
And the book of the sea is full of old-fashioned looks,
Some of which can kill, and very probably will,
Or make a seafarer sea-sick and occasionally ill.

But one can also become ill and die on land
Where there are no boats or ships to be manned.
Whether one lives or dies, one can do it just as well at sea,
Where intrepid seafarers take to the oceans and roam free.

We all want to know the purpose of our lives
And what, exactly, we are supposed to be doing here
On earth? And such questions and many more besides
Can be considered equally well at sea by those without fear
Of the answers to which they may have to lend an ear.

Poets read the sea
To write their poetry
And nobody ever died
Of a poem. Maybe they cried,
But they never died, did they?
It's hard to say,
But I think not,
Not that poetry lot!
They died of other things instead
And usually in a warm bed.

But many seafarers have lived to tell the tale
And, my God, they have told it remarkably well.
Is there any story better than the tale of the sea?
Not according to most seafarers who have spoken to me.
As for this book, you'll have to wait and see,
Until you've got to the end of it,
Whenever you see fit.

*Bob Crew*

## QUIETLY PROUD

When we talk of England's astonishing naval history
And sing of its many seafaring adventures, in poetry,
There is so much of which to be quietly proud.
Not foolishly or out loud proud,
But gently and quietly,
In the interests of accuracy.

The same is also true of the USA,
As will be seen in this startling array
Of sea poems from both sides of the pond
Where Brits and Americans have been equally fond
Of the inescapable and ever challenging sea.
Hence this marathon anthology.

This is a book for seafarers all
Who respond to the irresistible call
Of the sea, whether full or part time,
As they take to the whispering and secretive brine
That has such an intriguing story to tell
As the oceans roar and the seas swell.

So let us in these pages be quietly proud
And celebratory, but not out loud.

*Bob Crew*

# JOHN MASEFIELD
## Old man from the sea

I f anyone is the seafarers' poet, it is the English Poet Laureate and former merchant seaman, John Masefield (1878–1967). This opening showpiece section is devoted exclusively to the precious and magical works of this writer, whom I have nominated the 'old man from the sea', claiming that the best of his reality poems have about them the freshness of newly picked flowers.

For me – and no doubt for others too – he is an all-time favourite. He is, perhaps, the grandfather of modern sea poetry in Britain, writing largely factual poems, of gritty realism, but in many cases with such a rare and astonishing lightness of touch – and a breezy, versifying style, all his own – that we are instantly captivated and swiftly transported to England's coastal ports and beaches where we can take the sea air (fill our lungs with it), smelling the salt in the atmosphere, and feeling the ripple in the waves (we are also transported to foreign climes and shores). Masefield is a strikingly atmospheric and musical poet who charms and refreshes us with the gentle music of the sea and the invigorating smell of it, as he puts bounce into our step with his delightful rhythms, and pours magical light into the images that he conjures up, light such as we find in the best paintings that adorn the walls of our art galleries, the finest quality of which captures transient moods and moments in the life of the subject, the life of the sea and of seafarers in the case of Masefield's poetry. He is a true artist, perhaps the best sea poet that the English-speaking world has to offer, who sweeps us away with the lyrical ebb and flow of his moving poems, the best of which are almost Mozartian in the gentle way in which they bring the music and voice of the sea to our ears.

Not that all of Masefield's works were as gentle as those included in this collection of favourite poems, because he also wrote sea and other poetry in harsh and 'un-poetic' language that reflects the ugly realism of English country life as well as life at sea. Nor were they all factual, because he wrote many ballads. But, more than any other poet, the best of Masefield's sea poetry seems to me to sing out and speak for early- to mid-twentieth-century generations of Britons, for whom the Merchant and Royal Navy fleets were a major employer, and whose seafaring spirit of adventure is so brilliantly represented in the best of his works, which happen to be factual.

Here is a poet with a sailor's insight, who knew exactly what he was talking about, because he went to sea as a boy to become a cadet officer in the Merchant Navy – where he was appalled by the violence of the sailors, and from which he hastily departed because he suffered from sea-sickness! But he loved ships and the sea, for all that, in the days before passenger aircraft for the masses, when the only way to travel – or indeed to escape poverty at home in the back streets of Britain's inland towns and cities (Masefield's parents died when he was young) – was to go to sea, which Masefield did at the tender age of 13 years (others went into the army or down the mines). When he jumped ship in New York, he worked there in factories and bars, whilst reading as much as he could in order to improve himself and become a writer before he was through. And before he was through, this sensitive young man, without too much formal education, and for whom life was such a hard struggle – and who wrote such sensitive and perceptive poetry – finished up on the *Manchester Guardian* newspaper and as Britain's Poet Laureate from 1930 until his death in 1967. He was the longest-serving Laureate of all, except for Tennyson before him. By the time he died, this most prolific and energetic of writers had published twenty novels, eight plays (some in verse) and fifty books of poetry and verse.

There is a gentle and sometimes shaded radiance – and varying quality of light – in the best of Masefield's poetry that shines and mistily drifts and filters through his text, colouring and capturing so many transient moments and fleeting moods that would not be coloured and captured otherwise, that would not be evident were it not for the trick of light that he has been able to employ. Such poems are like very fine paintings, as we shall see from the following sample. In addition to the poems reprinted here, he wrote long narrative poetry and sea ballads – but, sadly, there is not space in an anthology of this sort for more than a handful of his poems.

Had it not been for Ramsay MacDonald, Britain's first Labour Prime Minister, Masefield may not have become poet laureate. But, as a socialist prime minister, MacDonald, to his eternal credit, was attracted to an ordinary man of the people whose life had been as much of a struggle as that of the majority of the British electorate – and this, of course, was Masefield.

But his poetry was anything but ordinary.

## SEA-FEVER

I must down to the seas again, to the lonely sea and the sky,
And all I ask is a tall ship and a star to steer her by,
And the wheel's kick and the wind's song and the white sail's
       shaking,
And a grey mist on the sea's face and a grey dawn breaking.

I must down to the seas again, for the call of the running tide
Is a wild call and a clear call that may not be denied;
And all I ask is a windy day with the white clouds flying,
And the flung spray and the blown spume, and the sea-gulls
       crying.

I must down to the seas again, to the vagrant gypsy life,
To the gull's way and the whale's way where the wind's like a
       whetted knife;
And all I ask is a merry yarn from a laughing fellow-rover,
And quiet sleep and a sweet dream when the long trick's over.

*This is certainly Masefield's best-known and best-loved poem and, like the others in this collection, it has such a freshness about it – a freshness of newly-picked flowers (or of clean sheets, for that matter). It is a purifying and cathartic freshness that makes us feel good, that enables us to breathe the clean air of the sea, and of poetry at its best. But things are not quite as they appear to be, and this is not such a romantic poem as it sounds, because, as we see from the final line of this 'sweet dream' of going to sea, the experience is not very romantic or dreamy at all. It is, rather, a 'long trick', the ugly reality of which, as we know, too often destroys the dream. It is typical of Masefield not to ignore reality when writing a wildly romantic poem about the irresistible romance and call of the sea, but at the same time not to spoil the romance or his poetic art by rubbing our noses in it, by punching us on the nose with it. This subtle poem is typical of his lightness of touch and when he talks of the sea as 'a wild call and a clear call that may not be denied', therein lies the paradox of the dream and the trick! This wild, clear call that may not be denied – this 'call of the running tide' – is also true of the running tide of Masefield's poetry with its 'white clouds flying', 'flung spray' and 'sea-gulls crying', which is why I regard his work, as already observed in the introduction to this section, as truly Mozartian in the gently classical music that it makes. Just as the poet tells us that the call of the sea may not be denied, we cannot deny Masefield or his poetry either. And with regard to the varying quality of light that is also mentioned in the introduction, we see here the difference between the 'grey mist' and 'the grey dawn breaking' and the 'lonely sea and the sky' (representing a different colour entirely), not to mention the suggestion of the crystal-clear light of that 'star to steer her by' and the light behind and between those 'white clouds flying'. This is a flying poem, the gentle colouring and varying light of which precisely captures the fleeting moods of so many fleeting moments and in such a few lines of magical text – from dawn to the passing clouds and the night sky that requires a star to show the way.*

## CARGOES

Quinquireme of Nineveh from distant Ophir
Rowing home to haven in sunny Palestine,
With a cargo of ivory,
And apes and peacocks,
Sandalwood, cedarwood, and sweet white wine.

Stately Spanish galleon coming from the Isthmus,
Dipping through the Tropics by the palm-green shores,
With a cargo of diamonds,
Emeralds, amethysts,
Topazes, and cinnamon, and gold moidores.

Dirty British coaster with a salt-caked smoke stack
Butting through the Channel in the mad March days,
With a cargo of Tyne coal,
Road-rails, pig-lead,
Firewood, iron-ware, and cheap tin trays.

———

*How this poem positively glitters and gleams with the varying light
of so many contrasting colours! Fleeting colours of precious stones and
jewels, different exotic woods, ivory, colourful birds and strange animals
in distant lands bathed in sunshine, bringing to mind their sparkling
clear blue seas. There is such a radiance here, in contrast to the grey,
cold light of the 'mad March days' of the British Isles, with its dark and
gloomy moods and colours of black coal, grey lead, dark brown and
perhaps even rusty iron, and potentially warming firewood, all
transported by Masefield's oh-so-famous 'dirty British coaster' with its
'salt-caked smoke stack'. The words that the poet has chosen to describe
this coaster have rung out like church bells in British ears for generations. Coasters still exist, but they are no longer dirty, because they are
sleek modern vessels driven by relatively clean diesel engines. But when
Masefield wrote this poem they were steam-driven and coal-burning,
so they were indeed dirty, and there was a sizeable fleet of them running
round the British Isles and across the English Channel. They had*

*columns of dirty black smoke billowing from their funnels – called smoke stacks by the Americans, which is doubtless where Masefield got the term, since he jumped ship in New York and worked there for a while.*

*Like 'Sea-fever', this is truly magical poetry of a very high order, with its compelling imagery and contrasting cargoes. It inspires seafarers to get into their boats and make off for sunny climes, whilst also tugging at their heartstrings with such homegrown images as the dirty British coaster. This is a homely, warming poem in a cold climate – with its firewood and coal – that crackles with poetic genius. But it is also a poem that reminds us of a world that is bigger than the tiny British world, as it embraces it with an alternative imagery. But we cannot have the one without the other, we cannot have the global sea power without the dirty coal that fuelled the coaster and the entire British economy at that time. How perceptive Masefield was and, again, such a lightness of touch in a poem that comes straight from the heart – a close second in the affections of the English to the poem 'Sea-fever'. What more can one say? What a poetic genius Masefield was.*

## TRADE WINDS
### (*from* Salt-Water Ballads)

In the harbour, in the island, in the Spanish Seas,
Are the tiny white houses and the orange-trees,
And day-long, night-long, the cool and pleasant breeze
    Of the steady Trade Winds blowing.

There is the red wine, the nutty Spanish ale,
The shuffle of the dancers, the old salt's tale,
The squeaking fiddle, and the soughing in the sail
    Of the steady Trade Winds blowing.

And o'night there's fire-flies and the yellow moon,
And in the ghostly palm-trees the sleepy tune
Of the quiet voice calling me, the long low croon
    Of the steady Trade Winds blowing.

*Seafarers will surely identify with the 'quieter voice' that calls them
during quieter moments out at sea when they have time to reflect on
their environment and what they are doing there. In this poem, it is the
voice of trade that is beckoning the poet and his sailor friends, although
I suspect that there is also the unmentioned and more spiritual voice of
poetry and reason calling him likewise. Linked with trade, there is, to
the good, the discovery of foreign culture, music, red wine, ale and
orange trees, all beckoning as a tantalising by-product of trade, and
then there is the story-telling of the seafarer in 'the old salt's tale', all
'soughing in the sail' of this delightful poem, which, again, subtly links
one thing with another: trade and its civilising by-products. What an
irresistible combination! One can well understand the tremendous pull
of Masefield's delicate poems to seafarers and the general public alike.
The call of the sea that he has to offer really is irresistible, especially
when you remember that these were days that did not know the relative
luxury or swift convenience of passenger and freight aircraft. And
again the light is filtering and drifting through, alternating the colouring
of this poem from the light of the yellow moon in contrast to the fireflies
and the 'ghostly' light of the palm trees that we can well imagine, and
perhaps even an orangey light from the orange trees in contrast to the
light of white houses – all different shades of light and colour with which
to explore and capture different moments and moods in this poem,
fleeting moments and moods before they pass and are lost forever –
one moment in the harbour, another with the dancers, the fiddler and
the storyteller, another among the palm trees, and another aboard
ship listening to the trade wind blowing.*

## THE WEST WIND
### *(an excerpt)*

It's a warm wind, the west wind, full of birds' cries;
I never hear the west wind but tears are in my eyes.
For it comes from the west lands, the old brown hills,
And April's in the west wind, and daffodils.

It's a fine land, the west land, for hearts as tired as mine,
Apple orchards blossom there, and the air's like wine.
There is cool green grass there, where men may lie at rest,
And the thrushes are in song there, fluting from the nest.

'Will ye not come home, brother? Ye have been long away,
It's April, and blossom time, and white is the may;
And bright is the sun, brother, and warm is the rain –
Will ye not come home, brother, home to us again?

―

*In contrast to 'Trade winds', this 'West wind' poem is a reminder to all seafarers and other travellers who roam far from home, how the homeland and the homestead beckons, however far away we may be. Strictly speaking this is not a sea poem, but it is a poem with the sea in mind. Even when seafarers are far out at sea, in hot pursuit of trade winds, they can never forget the haunting memories that are blowing in their direction from home, their songs 'fluting from the nest'. Yet again, Masefield links one thing with another – the call of the land with the call of the sea, travelling away from home whilst also being tugged and pulled at the heart strings back to it again. It is one thing to go away to sea, to escape from one's past or to get the landlubber's life out of your hair, but you can never get home, your past life and your homeland out of your system. And so Masefield's preoccupation with life's paradox – already referred to in the commentary on 'Sea-fever' – is in evidence again here. We are all torn, are we not, between travelling abroad and wishing to go home? And what a fine quality of light and colouring there is in this poem also, from that of the shaded 'old brown hills' to that suggested by the daffodils, in contrast to that of the 'bright sun' and the 'cool green grass' (at a time of day when the light is different than it is in the bright sunshine, of course), and the light of April in blossom time that is altogether different from other times when there is no blossom. And seafarers and travellers all can readily identify – can they not? – with 'hearts as tired as mine', fleetingly tired, or otherwise.*

## THE EMIGRANT

Going by Daly's shanty I heard the boys within
Dancing the Spanish hornpipe to Driscoll's violin,
I heard the sea-boots shaking the rough planks of the floor,
But I was going westward, I hadn't heart for more.

All down the windy village the noise rang in my ears,
Old sea-boots stamping, shuffling, it brought the bitter tears,
The old tune piped and quavered, the lilts came clear and strong,
But I was going westward, I couldn't join the song.

There were the grey stone houses, the night wind blowing keen,
The hill-sides pale with moonlight, the young corn springing green,
The hearth nooks lit and kindly, with dear friends good to see,
But I was going westward, and the ship waited me.

———

*In this sailor's song about the call of the sea that is, in many ways, breaking his heart – 'I hadn't heart for more', 'it brought the bitter tears' and 'I couldn't join the song' – one gets a feeling of the loneliness and isolation of he who goes to sea because there is a ship that 'waited me'. And we see that the call of the sea is not always very convenient for one who would like to join the dance and the 'hearth nooks lit and kindly, with dear friends good to see.' We also see, once again, the fine quality of varying light in Masefield's poetry, this time with dark hill-sides pale with the moonlight in contrast to the young corn springing green – capturing yet another fleeting moment and mood of 'pale' hillsides on account of the moon – and with the 'hearth nooks lit and kindly' inside the grey stone houses. And, as always, realism is not sacrificed to this poetic romance, because we have the 'sea-boots shaking the rough planks of the floor' to the accompaniment of Driscoll's violin and the Spanish hornpipes. Whilst this sea poem doesn't strike me as being in the same league as 'Sea-fever', 'Cargoes' or 'Trade winds', it does complete the picture of seafaring in a small sample of this kind. For me, Masefield's sea poems are insights – full of lightness and colour – into the seafaring life. But we are not quite finished yet!*

## TO THE SEAMEN

You seamen, I have eaten your hard bread
And drunken from your tin, and known your ways;
I understand the qualities I praise
Though lacking all, with only words instead,

I tell you this, that in future time
When landsmen mention sailors, such, or such,
Someone will say 'Those fellows were sublime
Who brought the Armies from the Germans' clutch.'

Through the long time the story will be told;
Long centuries of praise on English lips,
Of courage godlike and of hearts of gold
Of Dunquerque beaches in the little ships.

And ships will dip their colours in salute
To you, henceforth, when passing Zuydecoote.

———

*Masefield was right; the Dunkirk story is continuing to be told through the long time of history, echoing down the centuries, and this tribute poem shows him in a different light, as a war poet who is no longer concerned with the romance of the sea, but with its horror and misery instead, and with the quietly understated glory of British sailors. More than any other sea poet, he really does understand the qualities that he praises. But, while we see him in a different light, we also note the old-familiar lightness and brightness of touch ('hearts of gold', 'courage godlike', 'sublime', 'long centuries of praise', and ships that 'dip their colours in salute' – all bright colours and/or prospects to emerge out of the darkness of war).*

## THOUGHTS FOR LATER ON

When someone somewhere bids the bombing cease,
And ships unharassed ply at Life's demands,
And friends again greet friends in foreign lands,
And sad survivors call the ruin peace,

Then, peace will be but ruin, unless Thought
Of how the peace was purchased be in mind,
Of how, to buy it, men are lying blind
Under the sea in ruined wreckage caught;

Thinking of them, and of those who rode the air,
Or shogged the Flanders plain in Belgium's aid,
Or stood at Cassel with the grand Brigade,
Peace may be filled with beauty everywhere,

If, with each purchased breath, we vow to give
To Earth the joy they never lived to live.

Not any drums nor bugles with Last Post
For these men dead in intellect's despite.
Think not of war as pageant but as blight
Famine and blasting to the pilgrim ghost.

So, for the brave men fallen for man's crime
The young men beautiful all unfulfilled,
The broken and the mangled and the killed,
For whom no Spring can come in cuckoo-time,

Let there be beauty spilt like holy seed
Not any mock of custom or parade
But hope atoning for the ruin made
And shame alike for deed and want of deed.

———

*This is a very thoughtful and gentle poem of lament for the ugly game and shame of warfare, reminding us of the dire cost of war, not only at sea but in the air and on the land as well. It is also a poem about the need to repent and think again about the 'crime' of war that has sent so many to their death, as it urges us to give peace a proper chance in future, with the lines 'Peace may be filled with beauty everywhere / If, with each purchased breath, we vow to give / To Earth the joy they never lived to live.' The hope and expectation is that, by giving joy, we can create a beautiful and peaceful world in which there is no room for warlike hatred. Again, there is Masefield's characteristic brightness and light in evidence in this poem, with the light at the end of the tunnel that he creates out of bright 'beauty' and 'joy' and the 'cuckoo time' that is of course preferable to war, when 'friends again greet friends in foreign lands'. In contrast to the traditional 'pageant' of war, Masefield invites us to see it for what it is, a 'blight', a 'ruin' and a 'famine' that has denied brave men 'the joy they never lived to live'.*

## In conclusion

This sample of John Masefield's poetry is, of course, only a brief introduction to his works, but I hope that it may encourage seafarers to read more of his poems in future and – who knows? – perhaps to see them in a new light as a result of reading this book.

More than most poets in this collection, he voyages out rather than in, and is so delicately and pictorially descriptive, whilst also using light – by his use of words – to capture mood as well as image in his work, the fine texture of which is remarkable (not all pictorial or descriptive poems succeed in generating light and capturing mood). And the sensitive and subtle poems here tell of matters other than and, additional to, seafaring. They tell of beauty and art and poetry. Masefield is, for me, the Prince of Sea Poets, and I hope that readers like him too.

# THE BATTLE OF TRAFALGAR

W hen we read – as we do in this section – informational, factually based but opinionated poetry that has been written as a means of reporting and responding to historical events, and commenting upon them, we see how it differs from other more spiritual and intellectual forms of poetry. The difference lies either in the heavily detailed, highly descriptive and formal narrative – when we wonder how factually correct it is, or was (as it happens, these carefully researched poems are remarkably accurate) – or in the patriotic passion and praiseworthy eulogies on offer.

This is informative, openly conversational, journalistic poetry that is action-packed, and because it lacks a lightness of spiritual and emotional touch or purpose, it is obviously not as subtle or tenderly musical, or so gently pleasing to the mind, as some other forms of poetry. It may not reach the parts that other poems reach, or penetrate our deepest and most delicate feelings and innermost thoughts, putting us in touch with ourselves rather than the outside world. This is not to apologise for this style of informational and formal poetry, or the poetic commentary to which it gives rise; nor is it to say that it is not a legitimate and imaginative response to history and historical events that is not worth its place in this collection on merit – because it certainly is. But this is a more formal and factual sort of poetry. It is different from other more intimate and fictional/artistic forms, as it plays its creative and constructive part in vividly evoking past times and moods, and exposing us to them.

Some of these poems are naive and simplistic, while others are not, some are propagandistic, while others are not, as they take us on a journey into a lost world, whilst also illuminating and capturing the mood and perspective of that world, so that we can inhabit it, breathe its air, and feel how it felt. These are graphic, pictorial and rhythmic poems – some more architectural than they are spiritual or intellectual, more notable for the attitudes that they strike or for their craftsmanship than for their soulful or spiritual delicacy of feeling – and they are generally rousing and robust poems to sweep us off our feet and shake the dust from history, bringing it alive in this day and age.

The following is a sample of extracts from such works, old and new (some written with the benefit of hindsight, others not), commemorating Lord Nelson's victory at Trafalgar. As we read these poems from the perspective of the present, we can feel our spirits roused, as we take a quiet pride in our past, and feel relieved and grateful for it. These poems are of interest both to historians and to the general public. But because the Battle of Trafalgar was one of the biggest and most important sea battles of all time, they are of course of special interest to seafarers.

Whilst, predictably, this is the poetry of pride and prejudice and patriotism, it seems to me from the following examples that it is a quietly stated and not unintelligent pride, bearing in mind the awesome nature of the sea battle in question, and the subsequent threatened invasion of Britain by a mighty French army that was imminent and determined to crush the British. It stands to reason that if one man saves his country from such an unenviable fate – against the odds and perhaps even against all expectations – any poetry that is written about him will inevitably be the poetry of hero worship. In the poems in this section Nelson is conceived as a God of War, a thorn in the flesh, a saviour, a happy and fearless warrior, a warrior from heaven with a freshn'd soul who is 'hurled from the skies' to rescue his country, and as a reminder that it is 'no wonder England holds dominion o'er the seas', for as long as it has 'men like these'.

Not since Sir Francis Drake, who engineered the defeat of the Spanish Armada in 1588, had Britain seen anyone like Nelson. And, 200 years after the Battle of Trafalgar, who have we seen? Don't all reach for your pens at once.

## HE WAS A THORN IN OUR FLESH

'He was a thorn in our flesh,' came the reply –
'The most bird-witted, unaccountable,
Odd little runt that ever I did spy.'

*Robert Graves*

## DON JUAN

Nelson was once Britannia's God of War
    And still should be so, but the tide is turned;
There's no more to be said of Trafalgar.
    'Tis with our hero quietly inurn'd

*George Gordon, Lord Byron*

## ADMIRALS ALL

Admirals all, for England's sake
    Honour be yours and fame!
And honour, as long as waves shall break
    To Nelson's peerless name!

*Henry Newbolt*

## NATIONALITY IN DRINKS

Nelson for ever – any time
Am I his to command in prose or rhyme!
Give me of Nelson only a touch,
And I save it, be it little or much:
Here's one our Captain gives, and so
Down at the word, by George, shall it go!

*Robert Browning*

## HOME THOUGHTS, FROM THE SEA

Nobly, nobly Cape St Vincent to the North-west died away;
Sunset ran, one glorious blood-red, reeking into Cadiz Bay;
Bluish mid the burning water, full in face Trafalgar lay;
In the dimmest North-east distance dawn'd Gibraltar grand
      and gray;
'Here and here did England help me: how can I help
      England?' – say

*Robert Browning*

## CHARACTER OF THE HAPPY WARRIOR

Who doomed to go in company with pain,
And fear and bloodshed, miserable train!
Turns his necessity to glorious gain.

*William Wordsworth*

## GOD SAVE THE KING, 1803
### (*a lady's additional verse!*)

While war shall rage around,
May Nelsons still be found,
To guard our Isle.


## THE PHANTOM FLEET

As Nelson's calm eternal face went by,
Gazing beyond all perishable fears
To some imperial end above the waste of years.

*Alfred Noyes*


## ON THE BIRTHDAY OF ADMIRAL NELSON

What day more fit the birth to solemnize
Of the greatest hero you can surmise?
'Tis that consecrated to the Prince of Hosts
Of whose strong protection each Christian boasts.
That noble Nelson on this day was born
Most clearly showed he would the world adorn,
The warrior of Heaven, hurl'd headlong from the sky.

*Anonymous*

## TRAFALGAR
### (*an excerpt*)

'Twas at the close of that dark morn
    On which our hero, conquering, died,
That every seaman's heart was torn
    By stripe of sorrow and of pride.

Of pride that one short day should show
    Deeds of eternal splendour done –
Full twenty hostile ensigns low,
    And twenty glorious victories won:

Of grief, the deepest tenderest grief
    That he on every sea and shore –
Their brave, belov'd, unconquer'd chief –
    Should fly his master-flag no more.

*Anonymous*

## NELSON'S VISION

Blake and Rooke, and Vernon near him
    Crown'd with glory's laurel wreath,
Chase despairing thoughts, and cheer him
    On to victory or death.
Like a giant from his slumber,
    Swift he starts, with freshen'd soul;
Yes – among that sainted number
    Nelson shall his name enrol!

*H. L. Torre*

## TRIBUTE TO ADMIRAL HARDY

Upon a terrace by the Thames
 I saw the admiral stand,
He who received the latest clasp
 Of Nelson's dying hand.

Age, toil and care had somewhat bowed
 His bearing proud and high,
But yet resolve was on his lip
 And fire was in his eye.

I felt no wonder England holds
 Dominion o'er the seas,
Still the red cross will face the world
 While she hath men like these.

*Letitia Elizabeth Landon*

## NELSON: TERROR OF THE FRENCH

What a ghostly, eerie phantom
Horatio Nelson proved to be
To the haughty French.
He who sank their ships to the bottom
Of a hungry and unforgiving sea
That is such an unrelenting wrench
When it takes vessels steadily down
In their desperately angry frown
Of exasperated defeat,
That is so deliciously sweet
To their hated enemies,
For whom the defeated are short of remedies
That can save them from their misery
And the prolonged judgement of history.

How Villeneuve and Napoleon
Must have been haunted
By the invincible Nelson.
He who was never daunted
By a French or Spanish man of war,
Having defeated them both before,
From Italy and Egypt to Trafalgar
Without his foes becoming, evidently, any the wiser
About the development of his unconventional, cut and thrust
       style,
That lost the French Trafalgar after the Battle of the Nile.

Villeneuve, a born pessimist, with his 27 Franco-Spanish ships –
       seventeen of which
Were captured rather than sunk – was completely
       outmanoeuvred by
Nelson's fancy footwork, as the brilliant and optimistic
       Englishman broke all the rules,
As he had done before in the Italian campaign, getting in close
       and fearless

In two columns, slicing through Villeneuve's fleet, like a knife
      through butter,
Splitting it into three and getting under its long guns to the
      disbelief of the Frenchman
Who, after the battle, sadly committed suicide out of deep
      remorse.

Having to encounter Nelson on the high seas was a real bitch
In those far off times, when his startled enemies wondered why
They could never defeat him, as he made them all look like fools.
With his extraordinary and astonishing tactics –
That he employed with peerless daring and arrogance –
He implemented his heroic do-or-die plan
That wrecked the French fleet and was such a drain on
      Napoleon's purse.

What was it with Napoleon, could he really not see
That it was impossible to defeat Nelson of the Royal Navy?

Or was *that* it?
The prospect of achieving the impossible?
If so, what a blue and frenzied fit
He must have had when he was rendered completely risible
By Nelson, overlord of the sea, and of the over-weening French
Who never recovered from the echoing sound and ghastly
      stench
Of humiliating defeat
That was so sweet
To English nostrils and ears,
Not least in future years.

We can still smell and hear it all now
In the new millennium,
If we know how
To read the compendium
Of informative sea poetry
That is sometimes the first narrative of history.

Make no mistake about it! This was an all-important battle that
      most historians think
Had Britain with its back against the wall, as it teetered
      precariously on the brink.

When Nelson defeated his formidable foe in the Med, between
      Cadiz and Gibraltar,
It ended the ominous threat of an invasion of England by a
      mighty French army,
Whilst also ensuring that the English-speaking world, including
      North America,
Would be English rather than French or Spanish speaking.
It was at glorious Trafalgar
That Nelson sent a signal that, in this day and age, probably
      sounds a trifle barmy,
Which was, wait for it, 'England expects that every man will do
      his duty', yes sir!

It was brave Nelson who made heroism into a spellbound duty
That served Britain and its Empire well in future years,
Lending to the heroic a certain romance and beauty
That charmed the masses even when it ended in acid tears.

How well it worked then, as it worked for Drake in the defeat of
      the Spanish Armada,
And who is to say that it wouldn't work again if –
      and we would all, of course, rather
Not think about it – but if there was another threat of invasion
      from any quarter,
Who is to say that it wouldn't work for every man and wife, son
      and daughter?

It was Trafalgar that established British naval supremacy of the
      high seas
Until, a century and more later, the United States of America
      took over

Where Britain left off, leaving British naval traditions to
      consistently breeze
Through red white and blue American flags and sentiments that
      were all in clover.

And it was at Trafalgar – mired by Nelson's death, reportedly by
      a French sniper –
Where the French met their other Waterloo, so decisively, two
      hundred long years ago
That have almost been erased by history's ceaseless windscreen
      wiper,
Except for the intervention of this year's bicentenary – to which
      all should go
In the age of global air rather than sea transport and battles in
      the new millennium –
To contemplate Nelson and history's swinging pendulum,
And to think about this handsome, one-eyed, one-armed man,
Who gave so much for his embattled country,
And to his mistress, Lady Hamilton, who apparently turned him
      into a Peter Pan
Of the bedroom, even though she finished up in dire poverty,
Dying destitute, in a poor house in Calais
(So what does that say?).

And, as the British look up to the top of Nelson's Column, in
      London's Trafalgar Square,
Seeing his closeness to an ocean of heaven and the gods that
      supposedly hover there,
They cannot but fail to wish him, oh so well,
Trusting that he is in heaven rather than hell,
Trusting that his battles were not in vain,
Trusting that they will never be called upon again
To defend their precious island shores
To settle history's seemingly impossible scores.

The British Admiralty was riddled with jealousy in those far-off
       days,
Which is why Nelson had his enemies at home as well as abroad.
But he was more popular with the masses whose admiration was
       all-ablaze
For intrepid Nelson, more than any other war hero, as they
       thanked the Lord
For Horatio and took to the streets to cheer him wherever he
       went,
Leaving the carping of his critics utterly mis-spent.

Of course, Nelson was no doubt more vain and arrogant
Than the French themselves,
       and that can be taken as a compliment
By Britain's Gallic friends across the English Channel,
Who are entering into the spirit of this year's Bicentenary
       celebrations.
They are sending yet another French fleet
For the British to meet,
This time as genuine friends, rather than implacable foes,
Which is infinitely better, as every enlightened thinker knows.

Ships from all over the world will join Britain's magnificent
       Royal Navy
In its 600-year-old tradition of the fleet review, turning this into
       a modern symbol
Of maritime friendship and co-operation that is truly
       international and inspirational,
So three cheers, indeed, for the Royal Navy!

But most of all, all hail to Nelson, and thank you too,
What would Britannia have done without you?

And thank you Mrs Nelson, sexually neglected as you obviously
      were.
We don't doubt that Emma Hamilton  must have caused a
      painful stir.
And thank you British sailors all
Who rallied to Nelson's call.

*Bob Crew*

# EMILY DICKINSON

I n this sample of the poetry of Emily Dickinson (1830–1886), we see that her work is not about seafaring or the sea, but that it is about 'a maritime conviction in the atmosphere'. Here is a nineteenth-century landlubber who was wide open to the sea and to seafaring – and her poems are about how she feels and thinks about these matters – and for someone who did not go to sea, it is remarkable how much and how often she thought, felt and wrote about it. On the other hand, without seafaring and the aptly named maritime conviction to which she referred – without a sea of faith, as it were – there would have been no United States of America. So the powerful psychological impact of seafaring on American poets is entirely understandable. It is also understandable in their British counterparts, who could not begin to imagine an outside world without first imagining the sea that surrounded their island and the seafarers who eventually tamed it most of the time. So they, too, were just as reliant on seafaring and maritime convictions as their American cousins, for much of their poetry. It was seafaring and the sea that was informing poetry, which in turn informed seafarers back again, with a thought-provoking narrative all its own.

But it is the poet's perspective, not the seafarer's, that we have in the poetry of Emily Dickinson, with such tantalising suggestions as 'there is no frigate like a book' – nothing to compare with mind travel, not even sea travel. Yet, at the same time, there is her maritime conviction in the atmosphere, so the two would seem to be well matched – a meeting of minds.

The interesting thing about this is how seafaring and the sea, throughout the history of Britain and America, have never failed to inspire the creative imagination of poets and influence their thought processes, have never failed to help shape British and American culture. With or without realising it, seafarers, by reason of what they do, have put their stamp on our culture and inspired great works of art.

Emily Dickinson's is lightness-of-touch poetry, gesturing towards imagism – absolute precision in the presentation of the individual image – and controlled free verse as opposed to 'mere' description (of which she and other American poets, such as Ezra Pound, were contemptuous). We can see in her poetry how sea imagery influences her inner thoughts, as she not only borrows from the sea, but tames it too!

She is a tight-lipped, aphoristic writer – forever looking for maxims and wise sayings – who turns the perceived 'wisdom' of sea into a well-mannered gentlemanly visitor that is obedient and respectful and perhaps a suitor or lover to whom her heart goes out. She is, in many ways, Henry James's Isabel, in *Portrait of a Lady*, but with a good head and heart for poetry. And she observes that 'the brain is deeper than the sea', which is of course true, but then again, the sea, aided by global warming, may have the last laugh (see 'When the sea strikes back' on page 130) – not that she would have known about this at the time.

The daughter of a seriously strict Calvinist, Emily locked herself up in her bedroom (out of sight and mind, as if at sea) for most of her adult life, usually dressed in white – like a puritanical White Muslim. Perhaps only two of about 1,775 poems and fragments written by her were published in her lifetime. One can reasonably say that hers was a nineteenth-century American voice lost at sea.

She led a solitary and sternly disciplined life in which she was

> Tried always and Condemned by thee
> Permit me this reprieve
> That dying I may earn the look
> For which I cease to live –

This is presumably a reference to her tyrannical and religious father, whose religious belief she did not share.

Emily's is essentially introspective and purist poetry – much of which is fragmented, or fragments of disembodied poems – and it is gently soulful, spiritual and sexual. It is also the poetry of ideas. Her concept, in the following poems, of a period of several seas as a presumption of eternity is an interesting one. So, too, is her concept of hope being shipwrecked in the mind. Although she voyages out, just a little, with her dog, or on a beach, she soon withdraws into her inner self, whereupon she quickly closes the door. Compared to only a handful of sea poems and other references in her works, there are more than fifty poems and references on the subject of the human soul alone. So she is clearly much more preoccupied with the voyage in than the voyage out. Whilst her poetry is not inaccessible, it is not entirely open or accessible either, but somewhere in between. But most of her images are clear and bright, as they flit around like dragonflies on a pond, and there are some sumptuous moments to be enjoyed.

But this is also jerky brush-stroke poetry, in dabs and splashes of colour, often without full stops on the printed page – it is interspersed with lots of very eccentric dashes instead – and it has too many irritating capital letters for my liking, although, as the English poet Ted Hughes has pointed out, this is clearly an integral part of her method and style. Emily or her publisher misspells ankle (I mention these things for those readers who may wonder about spelling mistakes in this book) and, because of the occasional esoteric and enigmatic nature of her poetry – aided by unconventional punctuation without commas or semi-colons – it is easy to lose the plot in some poems (this is a poet for whom plot is by no means the important thing, as she reflects the riddle and mystery of life in her electrically charged poetry). Of course, Emily was trying to turn back the tide of conventional poetry when she put pen to paper, and there is a deliberate and studied incompleteness about her work, much of which may strike one as being unfinished (hence the use of so many dashes and an absence of full stops in her method and style). It is as if a finished and/or polished poem was not good enough for her, as if she was trying to comment on poetry itself by the unconventional way in which she structured and wrote it – 'True Poems flee,' she observes in her poem 'To see the Summer Sky' – it is as if some of her poetry is fleeing from her, not infrequently leaving behind an image of a poem, rather than a complete poem in the traditional sense.

> To see the Summer Sky
> Is poetry, though never in a book it lie –
> True Poems flee –

There is a fleeting quality in this poetry, which, at its best, makes its point without labouring the point, as imagery takes over from description. Like a painter dipping into the sea, as if it were a pot of paint, she daubs her egocentric canvas with different sea images and colours. The sea is representative of her poetic imagination. What she perceives in the universe – the sea, the cosmos – fills her with awe. One cannot read her sea poetry without realising that her imagination is absolutely flooded and engulfed by the awesome nature and timeless 'deep eternity' of the sea and what the seafarers are managing to do with it.

Because she shunned openly descriptive poetry, her descriptions and thought processes are to be found in the riddle of her nakedly revealing images, the inner meanings of which are mostly internalised (and because her poems are untitled, I have, for clarity of purpose and ease of reference, turned her first lines into titles).

Seafarers will be only too familiar with the 'solitude of sea' to which Emily Dickinson refers, as she reflects upon other solitudes besides – including the solitude of a soul admitted to itself in the penultimate poem in this sample – and they may even remember the 'divine intoxication' of those who go to sea for the first time, taking an 'inland soul to sea', as Emily Dickinson puts poetry into the soul of seafaring in no uncertain manner.

Her poem 'There is no Frigate like a Book' – 'to take us Lands away' – reminds us of the relationship between thought and action in this life, and, more to the point from the perspective of seafarers, that there would have been precious little to put into 'travelling' books of sea poetry and/or fiction without the seafaring explorers and men of action who came before the printed words that followed most of their exploits. We are reminded of the symbiotic relationship between writing about things and doing them, and how the two have can come together in books of sea poetry, how they benefit each other.

Emily Dickinson was brought up in a world in which seafaring was not only all the rage, but all the conversation as well in so many homes and drawing rooms, so it is hardly surprising that it captured – flooded – her imagination as much as it did. If it were not for seafaring there would have been no United States of America, so from the word go it has haunted the American poetic imagination.

## AN EVERYWHERE OF SILVER

> An Everywhere of Silver
> With Ropes of Sand
> To keep it from effacing
> The Track called Land.

## DOWN TIME'S QUAINT STREAM

> Down Time's quaint stream
> Without an oar
> We are enforced to sail
> Our Port a secret
> Our Perchance a Gale
> What Skipper would
> Incur the Risk
> What Buccaneer would ride
> Without a surety from the Wind
> Or schedule of the Tide –

## THERE IS NO FRIGATE LIKE A BOOK

There is no Frigate like a Book
To take us Lands away
Nor any Courses like a Page
Of prancing Poetry –
This Travel may the poorest take
Without offence of Toll –
How frugal is the Chariot
That bears the Human soul.

## IF WRECKED UPON THE SHOAL OF THOUGHT

If wrecked upon the Shoal of Thought
How is it with the Sea?
The only Vessel that is shunned
Is safe – Simplicity –

## I THINK THAT THE ROOT OF THE WIND IS WATER

I think that the Root of the Wind is Water –
It would not sound so deep
Were it a Firmamental Product –
Airs no Oceans keep –
Mediterranean intonations –
To a Current's Ear –
There is a maritime conviction
In the Atmosphere –

## WATER MAKES MANY BEDS

Water makes many Beds
For those averse to sleep –
Its awful chamber open stands –
Its Curtains blandly sweep –
Abhorrent is the Rest
In undulating Rooms
Whose Amplitude no end invades –
Whose Axis never comes.

## THE MOON IS DISTANT FROM THE SEA

The Moon is distant from the Sea –
And yet, with Amber Hands –
She leads Him – docile as a Boy –
Along appointed Sands –

He never misses a Degree –
Obedient to Her Eye
He comes just so far – toward the Town –
Just so far – goes away –

Oh, Signor, Thine, the Amber Hand –
And mine – the distant Sea –
Obedient to the least command
Thine eye impose on me –

## THE DROP, THAT WRESTLES IN THE SEA

The Drop, that wrestles in the Sea –
Forgets her own locality –
As I – toward Thee –

She knows herself an incense small –
Yet *small* – she sighs – if A*ll* – is A*ll* –
How *larger* – be?

The Ocean – smiles at her Conceit –
But *she*, forgetting Amphitrite –
Pleads – 'Me'?

## MY RIVER RUNS TO THEE

My River runs to thee –
Blue Sea! Wilt welcome me?
My River waits reply –
Oh Sea – look graciously –
I'll fetch thee Brooks
From spotted nooks –
*Say* – Sea – Take *Me*!

## I STARTED EARLY – TOOK MY DOG

I started Early – Took my Dog –
And visited the Sea –
The Mermaids in the Basement
Came out to look at me –

And Frigates – in the Upper Floor
Extended Hempen Hands –
Presuming Me to be a Mouse –
Around – upon the Sands –

But no Man moved Me – till the Tide
Went past my simple Shoe –
And past my Apron – and my Belt
And past my Boddice – too –
And made as He would eat me up –
As wholly as a Dew
Upon a Dandelion's Sleeve –
And then – I started – too

And He – He followed – close behind –
I felt His Silver Heel
Upon my Ancle – Then my Shoes
Would overflow with Pearl –

Until We met the Solid Town –
No One He seemed to know –
And bowing – with a Mighty look –
At me – The Sea Withdrew –

## THE BRAIN IS DEEPER THAN THE SEA
### (*an excerpt*)

The Brain is deeper than the sea –
For – hold them – Blue to Blue –
The one the other will absorb –
As Sponges – Buckets – do


## A SLOOP OF AMBER SLIPS AWAY

A Sloop of Amber slips away
Upon an Ether Sea,
And wrecks in Peace a Purple Tar,
The Son of Ecstasy –


## AS IF THE SEA SHOULD PART

As if the Sea should part
And show a further Sea –
And that  – a further – and the Three
But a presumption be –

Of periods of Seas –
Unvisited of Shores –
Themselves the Verge of Seas to be –
Eternity – is Those –

## IT TOSSED AND TOSSED

It tossed – and tossed –
A little Brig I knew – o'ertook by Blast –
It spun – and spun –
And groped delirious, for Morn –

It slipped – and slipped –
As One that drunken – stept –
Its white foot tripped –
Then dropped from sight –

Ah, Brig – Good Night
To Crew and You –
The Ocean's heart too smooth – too Blue –
To break for You –

## THE HEART HAS NARROW BANKS

The Heart has narrow Banks
It measures like the Sea
In mighty – unremitting Bass
And Blue Monotony

Till Hurricane bisect
And as itself discerns
Its insufficient Area
The Heart convulsive learns

That Calm is but a Wall
Of unattempted Gauze
An instant's Push demolishes
A Questioning – dissolves.

## A GREAT HOPE FELL

A great Hope fell
You heard no noise
The Ruin was within
Oh cunning wreck that told no tale
And let no Witness in

The mind was built for mighty Freight
For dread occasion planned
How often foundering at Sea
Ostensibly, on Land

A not admitting of the wound
Until it grew so wide
That all my Life had entered it
And there were troughs beside

## SWEET PIRATE OF THE HEART

Sweet Pirate of the heart,
Not Pirate of the Sea,
What wrecketh thee?
Some spice's Mutiny –
Some Attar's perfidy?
Confide in me.

## A SOFT SEA WASHED AROUND THE HOUSE

A soft Sea washed around the House
A Sea of Summer Air
And rose and fell the magic Planks
That sailed without a care –
For Captain was the Butterfly
For Helmsman was the Bee
And an entire universe
For the delighted crew

## THE SEA SAID 'COME' TO THE BROOK

The Sea said 'Come' to the Brook –
The Brook said 'Let me grow' –
The Sea said 'Then you will be a Sea –
I want a Brook – Come now'!

The Sea said 'Go' to the Sea –
The Sea said 'I am he
You cherished' – 'Learned Waters –
Wisdom is stale – to Me.'

## FORTITUDE INCARNATE

Fortitude incarnate
Here is laid away
In the swift Partitions
Of the awful Sea –

Babble of the Happy
Cavil of the Bold
Hoary the Fruition
But the Sea is old

## EDIFICE OF OCEAN

Edifice of Ocean
Thy tumultuous Rooms
Suit me at a venture
Better than the Tombs

## THERE IS A SOLITUDE OF SPACE

There is a solitude of space
A solitude of sea
A solitude of death, but these
Society shall be
Compared with that profounder site
That polar privacy
A soul admitted to itself –
Finite Infinity.

## EXULTATION IS THE GOING

Exultation is the going
Of an inland soul to sea –
Past the houses – past the headlands –
Into deep Eternity!

Bred as we, among the mountains,
Can the sailor understand
The divine intoxication
Of the first league out from land?

# WALT WHITMAN

I n contrast to Emily Dickinson, the sea poetry of the
American poet Walt Whitman (1819–1892) voyages
out and boldly so. It speaks directly rather than
indirectly of the sea and of seafaring, and is both descriptive
and accessible (rather than imagist and possibly inaccessible
therefore), using poetic language openly and conventionally,
instead of attempting to use imagery as a language and landscape of its own, in an unconventional manner, as Dickinson
did. Whilst Whitman's poetry is unorthodox in the sense that
it disregards meter, it remains quite conventional for all that,
and it is very descriptive (albeit with the bump and thump of
too many melodramatic exclamation marks, for my liking!). So
Whitman could not be more different from Dickinson, and his
robust and manly sea poems are specifically about the sea and
the practicality of seafaring, about the landscape of the sea,
whereas, as we have seen, Dickinson's sea poems are almost
entirely about how she feels about the sea, demonstrating how
she uses its imagery to voyage in and to explore the landscape
of her own inner self. Unlike Dickinson, Whitman does not
generally use sea imagery for that purpose (he may use other
imagery to explore his inner self, but not sea imagery), and
the maritime perspective that he has to offer is very much
the practical and uncomplicated perspective of the seafarer,
capturing the mood and adventurous spirit of life at sea, as well
as the significance and mystery of naval and sea power (in one
of the following poems he says that he would barter all of the
greatest poets and storytellers in return for an understanding
of the mystery of the sea).

With common consent, Whitman was regarded in the
United States as 'the bard of republicanism', and, as such, much
of his poetry is concerned with the equality of people and the
love of comrades (by contrast, Emily Dickinson was cut off from
and avoided society much of the time, as a result of which she

was a much more isolated and distant observer, but with a unique perspective all her own).

In his gritty and sometimes brash sea poems, Whitman rolls his sleeves up and embraces the big wide world in a big-hearted way, whereas Emily Dickinson's drawing-room poetry tends to view the sea from a discreet distance, through the window, or from a stroll on the beach (she is, perhaps, the Jane Austen of the world of American poetry). Whitman also had a somewhat idealised, perhaps naive, notion of international brotherhood between nations at sea – 'a pennant universal' over 'all seas and ships' – and 'one flag above the rest for the soul of man'. As can be seen from the following sample, this is clearly reflected in his works, which have concerned themselves with 'a spiritual woven signal for all nations' among the sea's 'separate flags of nations'. And he propounded the interesting concept of the ship aboard the ship and 'the ship of the soul'. Like Dickinson, Whitman put the soul into seafaring, and he also developed the idea of a book as an ocean-going vessel, but his is a much more practical book that voyages out rather than in.

Whitman was a journalist – in New York and elsewhere in the States – as well as a poet. He also worked as a carpenter, a country teacher and a government clerk for a while. In his *Leaves of Grass* he describes himself as: 'Walt Whitman, an American, one of the roughs, a kosmos ... eating drinking and breeding ... no sentimentalist.' During the American Civil War he was a war poet, who nursed his brother when he was wounded. He had Dutch–English racial origins. He was very much a man of action, who wrote action-packed poetry, and whilst he shared Emily Dickinson's concern for the sacredness of self and the beauty of the soul, there is not much of this to be found in his sea poetry, which is of the salty variety. Some of Whitman's non-sea poetry was considered too vulgar and immoral for the delicate sensibilities of many Americans at that time, for which the poet was fired by the US government for having published a book of immoral poems! In England, Whitman was becoming known in literary circles through the appreciation of an admirer, William Rossetti, the pre-Raphaelite art critic and author (brother of the famous artist), who was doubtless considered to be immoral himself.

Because Whitman's poems are conventional, accessible and informational, they require less explanation than Dickinson's, and he has a passion for seafaring that is hard to beat. The following is a sample of some of my favourites.

## CITY OF SHIPS

CITY of ships!
(O the black ships! O the fierce ships!
O the beautiful sharp-bow'd steam-ships and sail-ships!)
City of the world! (for all races are here,
All the lands of the earth make contributions here;)
City of the sea! city of hurried and glittering tides!
City whose gleeful tides continually rush or recede,
       whirling in and out with eddies and foam!
City of wharves and stores – city of tall facades of marble
       and iron!
Proud and passionate city – mettlesome, mad, extravagant
       city!
Spring up O city – not for peace alone, but be indeed
       yourself, warlike!
Fear not – submit to no models but your own O city!
Behold me – incarnate me as I have incarnated you!
I have rejected nothing you offer'd me – whom you adopted,
       I have adopted,
Good or bad I never question you – I love all – I do not
       condemn any thing,
I chant and celebrate all that is yours – yet peace no more,
In peace I chanted peace, but now the drum of war is mine,
War, red war is my song through your streets, O city!

## YOU TIDES WITH CEASELESS SWELL

You tides with ceaseless swell!  you power that does this work!
You unseen force, centripetal, centrifugal, through space's spread,
Rapport of sun, moon, earth, and all the constellations,
What are the messages by you from distant stars to us? what
      Sirius'? what Capella's?
What central heart – and you the pulse – vivifies all?  what
      boundless aggregate of all?
What subtle indirection and significance in you? what clue to
      all in you? what fluid, vast identity,
Holding the universe with all its parts as one – as sailing in a ship?

## IN CABIN'D SHIPS AT SEA

In cabin'd ships at sea,
The boundless blue on every side expanding,
With whistling winds and music of the waves, the large
      imperious waves,
Or some lone bark buoy'd on the dense marine,
Where joyous full of faith, spreading white sails,
She cleaves the ether mid the sparkle and the foam of day,
      or under many a star at night,
By sailors young and old haply will I, a reminiscence of the
      land, be read,
In full rapport at last.

*Here are our thoughts, voyagers' thoughts,*
*Here not the land, firm land, alone appears, may then by them*
      *be said,*
*The sky o'erarches here, we feel the undulating deck beneath our*
      *feet,*
*We feel the long pulsation, ebb and flow of endless motion,*
*The tones of unseen mystery, the vague and vast suggestions of the*
      *briny world, the liquid-flowing syllables,*
*The perfume, the faint creaking of the cordage, the melancholy*
      *rhythm,*
*The boundless vista and the horizon far and dim are all here,*
*And this is ocean's poem.*

Then falter not O book, fulfil your destiny,
You not a reminiscence of the land alone,
You too as a lone bark cleaving the ether, purpos'd I know
      not wither, yet ever full of faith,
Consort to every ship that sails, sail you!
Bear forth to them folded my love, (dear mariners, for you I
      fold it here in every leaf;)
Speed on my book! Spread your white sails my little bark
      athwart the imperious waves,
Chant on, sail on, bear o'er the boundless blue from me to
      every sea,
This song for mariners and all their ships.

## ABOARD AT A SHIP'S HELM

ABOARD at a ship's helm,
A young steersman steering with care.

Through fog on a sea-coast dolefully ringing,
An ocean-bell – O a warning bell, rock'd by the waves.

O you give good notice indeed, you bell by the sea-reefs ringing,
Ringing, ringing, to warn the ship from its wreck-place.

For as on the alert O steersman, you mind the loud admonition,
The bows turn, the freighted ship tacking speeds away under her
  gray sails,
The beautiful and noble ship with all her precious wealth speeds
  away gayly and safe.

But O the ship, the immortal ship! O ship aboard the ship!
Ship of the body, ship of the soul, voyaging, voyaging, voyaging.


## SONG FOR ALL SEAS, ALL SHIPS
### (*an excerpt*)

Flaunt out O sea your separate flags of nations!
Flaunt out visible as ever the various ship-signals!
But do you reserve especially for yourself and for the soul of man
  one flag above all the rest,
A spiritual woven signal for all nations, emblem of man elate
  above death,
Token of all brave captains and all intrepid sailors and mates,
And all that went down doing their duty,
Reminiscent of them, twined from all intrepid captains young
  or old,
A pennant universal, subtly waving all time, o'er all brave sailors,
All seas, all ships.

## THE WORLD BELOW THE BRINE

The world below the brine,
Forests at the bottom of the sea, the branches and leaves,
Sea-lettuce, vast lichens, strange flowers and seeds, the thick
tangle  openings, and pink turf,
Different colors, pale gray and green, purple, white, and gold,
the play of light through the water,
Dumb swimmers there among the rocks, coral, gluten, grass,
rushes, and the aliment of the swimmers,
Sluggish existences grazing there suspended, or slowly crawling
close to the bottom,
The sperm-whale at the surface blowing air and spray, or
disporting with his flukes,
The leaden-eyed shark, the walrus, the turtle, the hairy
sea-leopard, and the sting-ray,
Passions there, wars, pursuits, tribes, sight in those ocean-depths,
breathing that thick-breathing air, as so many do,
The change thence to the sight here, and to the subtle air,
breathed by beings like us who walk this sphere,
The change onwards from ours to that of beings who walk
other spheres.

## MIRACLES
### (*an excerpt*)

To me the sea is a continual miracle,
The fishes that swim – the rocks – the motion of the waves –
the ships with men in them,
What stranger miracles are there?

## WITH HUSKY-HAUGHTY LIPS, O SEA!
### (*an excerpt*)

Some vast heart, like a planet's, chain'd and chafing in those
   breakers,
By lengthen'd swell, and spasm, and panting breath,
And rhythmic rasping of thy sands and waves,
And serpent hiss, and savage peels of laughter,
And undertones of distant lion roar,
(Sounding, appealing to the sky's deaf ear – but now, rapport
   for once,
A phantom in the night thy confidant for once,)
The first and last confession of the globe,
Outsurging, muttering from thy soul's abysms,
The tale of cosmic elemental passion,
Thou tellest to a kindred soul.

## PROUDLY THE FLOOD COMES IN

Proudly the flood comes in, shouting, foaming, advancing,
Long it holds at the high, with bosom broad outswelling,
All throbs, dilates – the farms, woods, streets of cities –
   workmen at work,
Mainsails, topsails, jibs, appear in the offing – steamers'
   pennants of smoke – and under the forenoon sun,
Freighted with human lives, gaily the outward bound, gaily
   the inward bound,
Flaunting from many a spar the flag I love.

## HAD I THE CHOICE

Had I the choice to tally greatest bards,
To limn their portraits, stately, beautiful, and emulate at will,
Homer with all his wars and warriors – Hector, Achilles, Ajax,
Or Shakespere's woe-entangled Hamlet, Lear, Othello –
    Tennyson's fair ladies,
Metre or wit the best, or choice conceit to wield in perfect
    rhyme, delight of singers;
These, these, O sea, all these I'd gladly barter,
Would you the undulation of one wave, its trick to me
    transfer,
Or breathe one breath of yours upon my verse,
And leave its odor there.

## THE DISMANTLED SHIP

In some unused lagoon, some nameless bay,
On sluggish, lonesome waters, anchor'd near the shore,
An old, dismasted, gray and batter'd ship, disabled, done,
After free voyages to all the seas of earth, haul'd up at last
    and hawser'd tight,
Lies rusting, mouldering.

# RALPH WALDO EMERSON

I f, as already observed, Walt Whitman was 'one of the roughs', the nineteenth-century American poet Ralph Waldo Emerson (1803–1882) certainly was not. He was a Harvard-educated philosopher, essayist and poet, who gave up a ministership at the Old Second Church of Boston to formulate his own philosophy, which was chiefly characterised by its belief in intuition – 'trust thyself' and 'the divine sufficiency of the individual' – as the best way to comprehend and deal with reality, which is what his sea poems deal with. He was also a transcendentalist – 'the world is globed in a drop of dew' — and he even wrote a poem about 'Allah's love benign' for the sea. Emerson regarded life as a 'spiritual vision' and he was a smoother and more measured writer than either Dickinson or Whitman, more neat and tidy. His gentle poetry is brief and to the point, and is important to the historical development of the American seafaring narrative. Like Whitman – and unlike Dickinson – he deals in realism and he doesn't voyage into his inner self too much, at least not in his sea poetry. He voyages out, onto the high seas, believing – as he did in his philosophy of life – that each man has an Over Soul and that Nature is a Manifestation of spirit.

## I SPREAD MY GORGEOUS SAIL

I spread my gorgeous sail
Upon a starless sea
And o'er the deep with a chilly gale
My painted bark sailed fast & free –

Old Ocean shook his waves
Beneath the roaring wind,
But the little keel of the mariner braves
The foaming abyss, & the midnight blind.

The firmament darkened overhead,
Below, the surges swelled, –
My bark ran low in the watery bed,
As the tempest breath its course compelled.

I took my silver lyre,
And waked its voice on high; –
The wild blasts were hushed to admire,
And the stars looked out from the charmed sky.

Bear me then, ye wild waters,
To Apollo's Delphian isle,
My name is *Music*, in Castalie known,
Where bowers of joy the Nine beguile. –

## PLUNGE IN YON ANGRY WAVES

Plunge in yon angry waves,
    Renouncing doubt and care;
The flowing of the seven broad seas
    Shall never wet thy hair.

Is Allah's face on thee
    Bending with love benign,
And thou not less on Allah's eye
    O fairest! turnest thine.

## NORTHMAN

The gale that wrecked you on the sand,
It helped my rowers to row;
The storm is my best galley hand,
And drives me where I go.

## FROM ALCUIN

The sea is the road of the bold,
Frontier of the wheat-sown plains,
The pit wherein the streams are rolled,
And fountain of the rains.

## SEASHORE

Here chimes no clock, no pedant calendar,
My waves abolish time, dwarf days to hours,
And give my guest eternal afternoon.

# HERMAN MELVILLE

I If anybody was a man of the sea, the American
novelist, short-story writer and poet Herman Melville
(1819–1891) – author of *Moby-Dick* and *Billy Budd* –
certainly was. This is because he was a seafarer who voyaged all
over the place, including the South Seas, where he was reportedly captured by cannibals (who chose not to eat him for some
reason), and where he was later involved in a ship's mutiny. His
first voyage was to Liverpool in England, about which he wrote
a novel entitled *Redburn*. Having come from a prominent New
York family that fell on hard times, he went into the navy and
then turned his hand to farming, before he managed to bounce
back with the financial success of his novels and adventure
stories, but he went unrecognised by the American literati
(not until the 1920s did he win recognition, posthumously).
Although he was never rated as a poet in the United States, he
did write poetry, but he is better known for his other works
rather than for his poems. Even so, no anthology of sea poetry
can be complete without 'Father Mapple's hymn' from *Moby-
Dick*. Seafarers will readily understand how it feels to be in fear
of 'deepening down to doom.' And we are reminded of the disastrous fate of the *Titanic* in his poem 'The berg'.

## THE BERG (A DREAM)
### (*an excerpt*)

I saw a ship of martial build
(Her standards set, her brave apparel on)
Directed as by madness mere
Against a stolid iceberg steer,
Nor budge it, though the infatuate ship went down.
The impact made huge ice-cubes fall
Sullen, in tons that crashed the deck;
But that one avalanche was all –
No other movement save the foundering wreck.

FATHER MAPPLE'S HYMN
(*from* Moby-Dick)

The ribs and terrors in the whale,
    Arched over me a dismal gloom,
While all God's sun-lit waves rolled by,
    And lift me deepening down to doom.

I saw the opening maw of hell,
    With endless pains and sorrows there;
Which none but they that feel can tell –
    Oh, I was plunging to despair.

In black distress, I called my God,
    When I could scarce believe him mine,
He bowed his ear to my complaints –
    No more the whale did me confine.

With speed he flew to my relief,
    As on a radiant dolphin borne;
Awful, yet bright, as lightning shone
    The face of my Deliverer God.

My song for ever shall record
    That terrible, that joyful hour;
I give the glory to my God,
    His all the mercy and the power.

# HENRY WADSWORTH LONGFELLOW

O f all the nineteenth-century American poets in this collection, Henry Wadsworth Longfellow (1807–1882) is perhaps the most straight-laced and stuffy. He is also the most intellectual, moral and urbane. He is a decidedly literary poet who is likely to appeal to the reader who has a moral and intellectual relationship with the sea, as did he. But he was nevertheless a key player in the evolution of American sea poetry, having written some very orderly narrative poetry and ballads, in a smoothly lyrical and transparent style. Whilst his carefully controlled poetry is not particularly sharp, witty or imagist, it is perceptive from the somewhat lofty perspective of a New England university professor and translator, who studied European languages, having set sail for Europe often enough (the English poet John Betjeman wrote a poem about Venice dedicated to him).

Author of *Hiawatha* and other American mythologies, Longfellow wrote all sorts of poems of which the following on the subject of the sea are interesting examples, particularly those that remind us of the high-risk nature of nineteenth-century seafaring and deal with the subject of death at sea. Whilst Longfellow's use of imagery is not so dramatic or adventurous as – is more considered and restrained than – others, he nevertheless leaves us with some pleasing (intellectual) images, not the least of which are 'the inaccessible solitudes of being' (of which all long-distance seafarers will be only too aware) and 'the rushing sea-tides of the soul'. Whilst his poetry is not sprayed with the salt or heavy with the deep-sea atmosphere of the oceans – from which it seems to me that he manages to distance himself even when he is sailing on them – it is a thoughtful and intelligent response to seafaring.

## THE SOUND OF THE SEA

The sea awoke at midnight from its sleep,
    And around the pebbly beaches far and wide
    I heard the first wave of the rising tide
    Rush onward with uninterrupted sweep;
A voice out of the silence of the deep,
    A sound mysteriously multiplied
    As of a cataract from the mountain's side,
    Or roar of winds upon a wooded steep.
So comes to us at times, from the unknown
    And inaccessible solitudes of being,
    The rushing of the sea-tides of the soul;
And inspirations, that we deem our own,
    Are some divine foreshadowing and foreseeing
    Of things beyond our reason or control.

## THE LIGHTHOUSE
### (*an excerpt*)

The rocky ledge runs far into the sea,
    And on its outer point, some miles away,
The Lighthouse lifts it massive masonry,
    A pillar of fire by night, a cloud by day.

Even at this distance I can see the tides,
    Upheaving, break unheard along its base,
A speechless wrath, that rises and subsides
    In the white lip and tremor of the face.

And as the evening darkens, lo! how bright,
    Through the deep purple of the twilight air,
Beams forth the sudden radiance of its light
    With strange, unearthly splendor in the glare!

## SIR HUMPHREY GILBERT
(*an excerpt*)

Southward with fleet of ice
    Sailed the corsair Death;
Wild and fast blew the blast,
    And the east-wind was his breath.

His lordly ships of ice
    Glisten in the sun;
On each side, like pennons wide,
    Flashing crystal streamlets run.

His sails of white sea-mist
    Dripped with silver rain;
But where he passed there were cast
    Leaden shadows o'er the main.

Eastward from Campobello
    Sir Humphrey Gilbert sailed;
Three days or more seaward he bore,
    Then, alas! The land-wind failed.

Alas! The land-wind failed,
    And ice-cold grew the night;
And nevermore, on sea or shore,
    Should Sir Humphrey see the light.

He sat upon the deck,
    The Book was in his hand;
'Do not fear! Heaven is as near,'
    He said, 'by water as by land!'

In the first watch of the night,
    Without a signal's sound,
Out of sea, mysteriously,
    The fleet of Death rose all around.

## THE PHANTOM SHIP
*(an excerpt)*

A ship sailed from New Haven,
    And the keen and frosty airs,
That filled her sails at parting,
    Were heavy with good men's prayers.

'Oh Lord! if it be thy pleasure' –
    Thus prayed the old divine –
'To bury our friends in the ocean,
    Take them, for they are thine!'

But Master Lamberton muttered,
    And under his breath said he,
'This ship is so crank and walty,
    I fear our grave she will be!'

And the ships that came from England,
    When the winter months were gone,
Brought no tidings of this vessel
    Nor of Master Lamberton.

## From America – in conclusion

There are five American poets in this section who have, between them, written most of the most significant and memorable sea poems from the United States, demonstrating, it seems to me from the nature of their poetry, that they could not have written as much as they did without the necessary input from seafaring and seafarers. Space limitations have, alas, excluded Robert Frost, and there are doubtless other poets who have not caught my eye – some have, although they are not particular favourites of mine – but the poets here are those with whose sea poetry I am familiar, and who make the most sense to me in the context of this book. This is because they have influenced the genre more than others, and are likely therefore to be more interesting to seafarers. These are the American poets who have made the greatest contribution to sea poetry.

# *VOYAGING OUT*

T he remainder of this anthology, devoted to poets from Britain, is divided into three parts. In this first part there are open, accessible, outgoing and extrovert poems, poems that voyage out – onto the high seas and over the far horizon where poets unleash their imaginations on the subject of the sea and what is happening out there, what is to be found beyond it. Then in the second part there are the introspective poems that voyage inwards, into the inner thoughts of the poets when they write about things other than the sea, but still use the sea and its imagery. Finally there are voyaging-in-between poems, where poets do not quite make the journey out or in, but usually stay on the beach.

It is not easy to theme poems in this way, because of the marginal inward or outward nature of some of the poems in question. Even so, the attempt is worthwhile, because it helps us to see, not only how seafaring impacts on the minds and imaginations of poets, but also how marginal differences make a difference to the nature of the poem. So, much food for thought.

As we shall see, there is a psychological relationship between seafaring and the writing of poetry that favours the voyaging-out poems. But we shall also see how poets would not have been in a position to produce as many sea poems without the psychological dynamic that exists between seafaring and poetry, without the former being so active an influence on the latter. In this context, one can also see how, for example, the world of the seafarer has inspired the imagination of poets much more than, say, the world of medicine, or a goodly number of other areas of human endeavour. Seafaring is one of the greatest human-interest stories of all time, whether told in poetry or prose.

In this *Voyaging out* section there are poems of the wonders, journeys and terrors over the far horizon, and of the follies, pains and tragedies at sea.

## ULYSSES
### (*an excerpt*)

Come, my friends,
'Tis not too late to seek a newer world.
Push off, and sitting well in order smite
The sounding furrows; for my purpose holds
To sail beyond the sunset, and the baths
Of all the western stars, until I die.
It may be that the gulfs will wash us down;
It may be we shall touch the Happy Isles,
And see the great Achilles, whom we knew.
Tho' much is taken, much abides; and tho'
We are not now that strength which in old days
Moved earth and heaven, that which we are, we are, –
One equal temper of heroic hearts
Made weak by time and fate, but strong in will
To strive, to seek, to find, and not to yield.

*Alfred, Lord Tennyson*

## A VISION OF THE SEA
*(an excerpt)*

'Tis the terror of the tempest. The rags of the sail
Are flickering in ribbons within the fierce gale:
From the stark night of vapours the dim rain is driven,
And when lightning is loosed, like a deluge from Heaven,
She sees the black trunks of the waterspouts spin
And bend, as if Heaven was running in,
Which they seemed to sustain with their terrible mass
As if ocean had sunk from beneath them: they pass
To their graves in the deep with an earthquake of sound,
And the waves and the thunders, made silent around,
Leave the wind to its echo. The vessel, now tossed
Through the low-trailing rack of the tempest, is lost
In the skirts of the thunder-cloud: now down the sweep
Of the wind-cloven wave to the chasm of the deep
It sinks, and the walls of the watery vale
Whose depths of dread calm are unmoved by the gale,
Dim mirrors of ruin, hang gleaming about;
While the surf, like a chaos of stars, like a rout
Of death-flames, like whirlpools of fire-flowing iron,
With splendour and terror the black ship environ,
Or like sulphur-flakes hurled from a mine of pale fire
In fountains spout o'er it. In many a spire
The pyramid-billows with white points of brine
In the cope of the lightning inconstantly shine,
As piercing the sky from the floor of the sea,
The great ship seems splitting! it cracks as a tree,
While an earthquake is splintering its root, ere the blast
Of the whirlwind that stripped it of branches has passed.

*Percy Bysshe Shelley*

## KUBLA KHAN
### (*an excerpt*)

In Xanadu did Kubla Khan
A stately pleasure-dome decree:
Where Alph, the sacred river, ran
Through caverns measureless to man
    Down to a sunless sea.
So twice five miles of fertile ground
With walls and towers were girdled round:
And here were gardens bright with sinuous rills,
Where blossomed many an incense-bearing tree;
And here were forests ancient as the hills,
Enfolding sunny spots of greenery.

———

Through wood and dale the sacred river ran,
Then reached the caverns measureless to man,
And sank in tumult to a lifeless ocean:
And 'mid this tumult Kubla heard from far
Ancestral voices prophesying war!

*Samuel Taylor Coleridge*

## THE JOURNEY ONWARDS

As slow our ship her foamy track
    Against the wind was cleaving,
Her trembling pennant still look'd back
    To that dear isle 'twas leaving.
So loth we part from all we love,
    From all the links that bind us;
So turn our hearts, as on we rove,
    To those we've left behind us!

When, round the bowl, of vanished years
    We talk with joyous seeming –
With smiles that might as well be tears,
    So faint, so sad their beaming;
While memory brings us back again
    Each early tie that twined us,
O, sweet's the cup that circles then
    To those we've left behind us!

And when, in other climes, we meet
    Some isle or vale enchanting,
Where all looks flowery, wild, and sweet,
    And nought but love is wanting;
We think how great had been our bliss
    If Heaven had but assign'd us
To live and die in scenes like this,
    With some we've left behind us!

As travellers oft look back at eve
    When eastward darkly going,
To gaze upon that light they leave
    Still faint behind them glowing, –
So, when the close of pleasure's day
    To gloom hath near consign'd us,
We turn to catch one fading ray
    Of joy that's left behind us.

*Thomas Moore*

## JOHN HENRY'S RIVER

John Henry has gone across the English Channel to war-torn
       France
To build trusty bridges for British soldiers. He's with the Royal
       Engineers

During World War One, so there is of course always a chance
That he may not, alas, return, should his life end in tears.

He is a boat builder from the beautiful riverside village of
       Sonning on Thames,
A poetic river that not only flows out into the sea so majestically,
       but also wends

Its way inland, where John's boats have been in great demand.
But now that he has received the long-awaited command

To go to this beastly war,
He must close the door

For a while on the building of pleasure boats that he has crafted
       with such care.
He must go and build bridges instead, with which to pursue the
       enemy everywhere.

John Henry is a broad-shouldered, blue-eyed giant of a
       blond-haired man
And a half, who will not hesitate to kill as many of the enemy
       as he can.

He is a Warrior Sikh of the Anglo-Saxon race,
Who, predictably, will never disgrace

Himself or his country.
His beloved country.

He has sons in the Horse Guards and Cavalry and he will have
      grandsons as well
In the Marine Commando. Here is a man who will not flinch
      from the living hell

Of disgusting bloodshed and atrocious war
In a country where he's never been before.

In time he will have no-nonsense in-laws, too,  in the fearless
      Parachute Regiment,
This boat builder from a proud military family without any false
      or gooey sentiment

About what it takes to fight a brutal battle
When scintillating sabres furiously rattle.

This is the true and dignified character of fearless John Henry  Cole,
He who was a once-upon-a-time precious living soul.

But his brave heart was chiefly in boat building and rowing up
      and down
The leisurely River Thames, just a few miles outside Reading
      town.

He was a Berkshire man
And a proud Yeoman

Whose river flowed out to the inevitable sea
Where his spirit roamed alarmingly free.

'Rule Britannia! Britannia rules the waves!
Britons never shall be slaves.'

*Bob Crew*

## A WET SHEET AND A FLOWING SEA

A wet sheet and a flowing sea,
    A wind that follows fast
And fills the white and rustling sail
    And bends the gallant mast;
And bends the gallant mast, my boys,
    While like the eagle free
Away the good ship flies, and leaves,
    Old England on the lee.

O for a soft and gentle wind!
    I heard a fair one cry;
But give to me the snoring breeze
    And white waves heaving high;
And white waves heaving high, my lads,
    The good ship tight and free –
The world of waters is our home,
    And merry men are we.

There's tempest in yon hornéd moon,
    And lightning in yon cloud;
But hark the music, mariners!
    The wind is piping loud;
The wind is piping loud, my boys,
    The lightning flashes free –
While the hollow oak our palace is,
    Our heritage the sea.

*Alan Cunningham*

## THE CONVERGENCE OF THE TWAIN
*(an excerpt from lines on the loss of the Titanic)*

I

In a solitude of the sea
Deep from human vanity,
And the Pride of Life that planned her, stilly couches she.

II

Steel chambers, late the pyres
Of her salamandrine fires,
Cold currents thrid, and turn to rhythmic tidal lyres.

III

Over the mirrors meant
To glass the opulent
The sea-worn crawls – grotesque, slimed, dumb,
    indifferent.

IV

Jewels in joy designed
To ravish the sensuous mind
Lie lightless, all their sparkles bleared and black
    and blind.

V

Dim moon-eyed fishes near
Gaze at the gilded gear
And query: 'What does this vaingloriousness
    down here?'

*Thomas Hardy*

## CAPTAIN SMITH OF THE TITANIC

The late Captain Smith of the Titanic
Is putting Lizzie Sumnall in a panic.

He's taken her out to sea in a rowing boat
And a fierce storm has got them by the throat.

The captain is trying to get back to shore
With Lizzie, who's never been to sea before.

It's off the coast of Liverpool
And the captain's a bloody fool.

He's arrogant and listens to no one,
But this storm has got him on the run.

By the skin of his teeth, he just about manages to get back in
      time,
Before his fragile boat is upturned in the tempestuous brine.

Lizzie is seriously ill and, as for her fraught emotions, they
      are in a mess,
But the insensitive captain cannot understand why she's in
      such distress.

He was warned against his high-risk venture by ordinary
      seamen.
But, as usual, he would never ever listen to the likes of them.

They told him that an ugly and dangerous storm was brewing
But he insisted that he knew exactly what he was doing.

He and Lizzie would get back before the storm.
But now poor Lizzie is so desperately forlorn.

She'll not be seeing Captain Smith again
But she will never be able to forget his name –

Nor will the rest of us when the Titanic goes down,
All because this captain's been such an awful clown.

Captain Smith of the Titanic
Told Lizzie not to panic.

But now that this vainglorious captain's dead
And his proud and foolish character's been read,

We can see the nature of his awesome vanity
That was such a disastrous folly for those at sea.

In Captain Smith's care,
1,513 passengers and crew beware!

Unlike the arrogant captain, Lizzie lived to tell the tale.
She told it to her daughter Eileen, who told it to me as well.

*Bob Crew*

## A SONG IN STORM

Be well assured that on our side
    The abiding oceans fight,
Though headlong wind and heaping tide
    Make us their sport to-night.
By force of weather, not of war,
    In jeopardy we steer:
Then welcome Fate's discourtesy
    Whereby it shall appear
How in all time of our distress,
    And our deliverance too,
The game is more than the player of the game,
    And the ship is more than the crew!

Out of the mist into the mirk
    The glimmering combers roll.
Almost these mindless waters work
    As though they had a soul –
Almost as though they leagued to whelm
    Our flag beneath their green:
Then welcome Fate's discourtesy
    Whereby it shall be seen, etc.

Be well assured, though wave and wind
    Have mightier blows in store,
That we who keep the watch assigned
    Must stand to it the more;
And as our streaming bows rebuke
    Each billow's baulked career,
Sing, welcome Fate's discourtesy
    Whereby it is made clear, etc.

No matter though our decks be swept
 And mast and timber crack –
We can make good all loss except
 The loss of turning back.
So, 'twixt these Devils and our deep
 Let courteous trumpets sound,
To welcome Fate's discourtesy
 Whereby it will be found, etc.

Be well assured, though in our power
 Is nothing left to give
But chance and place to meet the hour,
 And leave to strive to live,
Till these dissolve our Order holds,
 Our service binds us here.
Then welcome Fate's discourtesy
 Whereby it is made clear
How in all time of our distress,
 As in our triumph too,
The game is more than the player of the game,
 And the ship is more than the crew!

*Rudyard Kipling*

## TROOP SHIPS ARE NO FUN

Sweaty troop ships are no fun
For hundreds of men in khaki
Who must sleep underneath
And on top of each other
In hastily erected dormitory hammocks,
Sharing the same stale and stifling air
Thick with farts, belches, and body odour,
And with nowhere to hang their sullied clothes.
But it's best not to talk about this in polite company.

I was once in the hot and dazzling Mediterranean sun
On such a cramped and hellish ship with the British Army,
Getting back to Blighty, gritting and grinding my teeth
When the men in khaki were pitched headlong and perspiring
　　　　　into another
Bothersome duty, this time in the rock-bottom ship's kitchens
　　　　　where many stomachs,
Hideously churning, were soon violently vomiting, much the
　　　　　worse for wear
After the guerrilla war on the beautiful Island of Love was
　　　　　finally over;
Heaving and vomiting because, as everybody who has been to
　　　　　sea knows,
In the queasy hold or galley of a deep-steep ship, stomachs
　　　　　cannot settle easily.

Down in the spiralling depths of such a distasteful ship, the toss
　　　　　and turn from the sea
Really is at its sickening worst for a shallow abdomen where, if
　　　　　you ask me,
No teenage soldier wanted to work a remorseless ten hours a day
On that oh-so-miserly pittance of 1950s National Service pay,
Cleaning out greasy-sleazy vats of remaindered food in the
　　　　　airless overheated kitchen,
Thinking and thinking of the freedom and freedom that had
　　　　　gone so sorely missing

In his young life.
But it's best not to talk about this in polite company
For fear of raising a grimy subject that may be considered too
    unseemly.

And then, back at Southampton, we discovered that the dockers
    were on strike,
And this was such bad news, because it soon put an untimely
    and sharp little spike
In our freedom-loving wheel when, instead of disembarking, we
    had yet another job to do,
Which was unloading the cargo for the ship's crew
That was anxious to get back to sea
And be shot of the men in khaki.

But eventually, when the time came for us to hitch a lift home at
    the roadside
From passing cars – because of those peanuts paid in the 1950s
    tight-fisted army –
We were free at last! Demob was just around the corner and the
    great wide
World of civilian life awaited us, but it's best not to talk about
    this in polite company.

This was, without doubt, the most disgusting and slavish sea
    journey of my life,
As we voyaged out into so much soul-destroying trouble and
    strife.

I feel this comfortless and lingering ache to this day,
Even though it is 45 long-gone, blood-sucking years away.

Some say it was character building
Rather than soul destroying
And I say it's best not to talk about it in polite company.

*Bob Crew*

## ACROSS THE SEA FROM INDIA

From India to England, through three vast oceans, really was the
    journey of a lifetime
For teenage Patricia, back in 1959, arriving on a grey day at
    Southampton in good time,
But with no one there to meet or greet her on the other side of a
    deep racial divide
Where she needed to discover if the natives were friendly, with
    her delightfully wide
Open smile and heart. She was among the first immigrants to
    come over the sea
From India's mixed-race Anglo-Indian community, this
    brown-skinned beauty
Who found, in due course, that friendly is what many of the
    natives certainly were.
But of others she was not quite so sure, not that she had ever
    cared to make heavy weather
About racial differences or those incurable birds of feather who
    always stick together.

But she was much loved and she soon integrated and married
    well,
So hers is a story of racial harmony and goodwill, of which to tell
Of a charming young woman whose warm heart and smile
    could always embrace
The entire universe and all the dividing oceans of the world, and
    melt the human race!

She married an Englishman
And had a daughter and son,
Having settled in London
According to her family's careful plan,
With all its members coming through
From Allahabad, one by one, and two by two.

They came into and out of their latter-day Ark
As casually as taking a stroll in the park

And there were other teenagers from India as well,
Including Armenian David from Calcutta – to dwell
Eventually in Reading – and Brahmin Ratan from Poona,
Also Reading bound, like those before him. No sooner
Than their feet hit the ground, when they first arrived,
They all found jobs from nine to five.

There was Brenda and Orville too,
June, Brian, Ronnie, Walter and Moira, to mention but a few.

And then there was Alice and her husband, Brian Senior,
Who came after their children, out of India's vast interior.

None was short of charm
With which to disarm

The natives, these strangers who came out of the sea on Britain's
          immigrant ships
With broad, broad smiles, and messages of good will on their
          lips,
These warm-hearted and intelligent people from hot India
Where they quickly made their mark in cold Britannia

Which was the other side of the moon then.
So here's to them and God bless them.

*Bob Crew*

## NOT ENOUGH SHIPS

If you are going to declare war on the world's biggest sea power,
It helps to have enough ships, Winston's Churchill's 'tools' to do
      the job.

But when the United States went to war with Great Britain
      during a dark hour
In our eighteenth-century history it soon found that it had trod

A hopeless seafaring path, because it simply didn't have enough
      craft
To take on the greatest sea power in the world. What a daft

Idea! So it got it into its defiant head
To raid British commerce ships instead

Of meeting battle ships head on in an outright war,
As it captured and destroyed British ships of commerce offshore.

Hostilities at sea had begun when the British seized
American ships that breezed

Across the Atlantic to trade with Napoleonic France.
There was, of course, no chance

That the British would tolerate this.
So they took care never to miss

An opportunity to imprison
American sailors on a trade mission

To France.
No chance!

But there was also no chance for Britain on far away US land
Where things did not go as the Old Country had planned.

How and why the British lost the war is no mystery
And the rest, as they say, is history.

Something like 40% of Americans were for the Old Country still,
As for the remainder, about half went off to Canada, leaving the
  will

Of the other half to prevail, eventually to become a sea power in
  their own right
That was more than capable, in future, of fighting the good fight.

*Bob Crew*

## A DRUG OF A HARBOUR

Where in this world will you find
Such a powerful drug of a harbour as this

That is busy, busy, busy
And dizzy, dizzy, dizzy

With so much coming and going in hectic action
Of the most incredible seafaring satisfaction?

You won't. There is nowhere to blind
You with such a frenzied maritime bliss

That delights and gladdens your heart
And blows your imagination wide apart

With stunning visual effects
That Mother Nature and modernity perfects.

This is adjective-defying territory of a kind that you have never
        seen
Before that is impossible to forget if you are lucky enough to
        have been

Here, letting your thoughts shoot the rapids of the striking
        spectacle before you
When you will surely have seen a great deal to thrill you (and to
        inform you, too).

Here is a *pulsating* astonishment that swamps and floods your
        mind
With every *swarming* image, shape, colour and extraordinary
        kind

Of ocean-going vessel, from the four corners of this mysterious
        and vibrant earth,

In an overflowing, multi-flagged and brightly-coloured cavalcade
      that is well worth

Seeing, and also feeling
To the root of your being.

Forget Naples, Venice, Istanbul, Cape Town, Lisbon
Athens, Shanghai and places like that. This is one

Magnificent city of ships of a completely different order
That is in every way more dramatic and bolder.

Forget Geneva with its lake and mountains,
Here is scenic beauty from strange and exotic fountains.

And this place is not just pleasing to the eye,
Which is how and why

It gets under your skin, in the tug and flood
And powerful undercurrent of your blood.

Here is a breath-taking harbour view to die for,
That will surely sink you. One can say no more.

This is a no-nonsense harbour that is seriously working
And where all sorts of other things are lurking.

And what there is to be seen here –
Whether from afar or up near –

Is beyond all imagining
And dreaming.

One cannot breathe the warm and humid air in these parts and
      fail to be uplifted
By all the cargoes, people and baskets of fish that are being so
      speedily shifted.

One cannot fail to be stung by the irrepressible verve of this
      everywhere atmosphere
That hangs in the drowsy air like sea salt and really is beyond
      compare.

There is an irresistible exuberance that you will not believe
And, sadly, a loss of history that Great Britain can never retrieve.

One cannot witness this floating maritime parade
Without feeling that you have made

It to somewhere quite overwhelmingly and hugely different
At this amazing gateway to a country in the world's largest
      continent.

So what's to see?
Harken to me.

What's to see is this: the biggest and best seaport in the Far East –
Once the third most important in Britain – where you can feast

Your eyes on an exciting seascape teeming with cargo ships,
      cruise liners, battleships,
And roll-on-roll-off ferries, all arriving in a deep-water shelter
      where the world tips

Its bounty into dockside warehouses called Godowns, as vessels
      come and go
All day long, one after the other and the other, in such an
      endless seafaring show

Complete with busy little tugs, fishing boats, Chinese junks and
      sampans,
And usually without mishap, because they are in safe and
      reliable hands.

All this glistening in the hot sunshine on a blue-green sea,
     including flying
Boats and speedboats taking themselves here and there.
It is of course mystifying

Where they all come from, or where they go
When they leave. Does anybody know?

There's a computerised control centre and harbour master, and
     a wide
Waterfront of cranes, derricks, cargo ships and dredgers, with a
     flowing tide

Of human traffic on sturdy old Red Star ferry boats, right out of
     the pages of history,
Safely shifting millions of new millennium people from one side
     of this divided city

To the other, for a few cents only. There are graceful yachts and
     sailing boats, dragon
Boats racing each other during annual festivals, and a discreet
     little sexual caravan

Of sampan brothels, surrounded by more dragon boats in
     training for their festivals,
Which is when dragon dances in this city's streets call for
     party-time rules.

Millionaires' junks follow a champagne picnic-route to the outer
     islands where
There are some of the best beachside fish restaurants in the
     world, and an air

Of supreme elegance and glamour is lent to this thriving scene
By these luxury craft, the like of which you will not have seen,

Some owned by companies for entertaining their VIP guests,
Others privately owned to feather rich nests.

There is a most extraordinary buzz about this place,
So, do yourself a favour, and make haste!
Police motor-launches and gunboats are also part of this lavish
      mosaic
Of naval history, geography and world shipping that is nothing
      less than a fantastic

Multi-national exhibition, spectacle and pageant; a grand and
      dazzling parade of ocean-
Going vessels, with a posh marina across the water, away from
      the commotion

Of the Chinese mainland opposite.
There's a lookout with a famous cannon gun
And sweeping panoramic vistas of mainland China.
There's also lots of downtown fun

In this aesthetically and commercially pleasing city, with all its
      many views
And its splendid gastronomic restaurants that are usually such
      good news.

Here lives Michele with her three children who attend the
      French School
Where they are generally well behaved, as a rule.

A Swiss-made cable car climbs like a sea snail up a flowered
      mountain peak
On one side of the harbour, while sea gulls and other birds with
      triumphant shriek

Swoop and dive into waves bursting with fish, boats and humanity
For all with an explosive eye for detail, with which to notice and
      see.

Cut me a slice of poetry!
Scoop me some more mystery.

Draw me a mental survey.
Paint me a picture today

(Some destinations and/or countries are intertwined with our
          unheralded fate
Without our knowledge, for a realisation of which we must
          patiently wait).

From the top of the mountain peak there are more astonishing
          views to be enjoyed
After the climbing cable car has, in the sweltering heat, been so
          usefully employed,

And there's a long suspension bridge at the distant waterfront
          end and two modern
Tunnels reaching out under ground, in which road vehicles
          disappear all of a sudden

Under the harbour to get to the other side
After an undersea ride.

There is even a street-side escalator of a pavement up a steep hill
          in the centre of town
That is protected from the wicked sun, with a canopy overhead,
          as it goes up and down.

And there are also some of the world's best and most luxurious
          hotels
And fashionable designer-shops all proudly looking on where
          the fleet sails.

As for the tube trains, so sharply efficient and pleasingly clean,
You will find none better wherever else you may have been.

The whole of this city and its surrounding territories is a shining
          example of engineering

At its very best. Carved out of rock and mountainside the
          achievement is staggering.

And out of this deep-water facility for massive foreign
          investment, global trade
And much East–West business, a towering skyscraper city has
          been made.

It has emerged out of harbour profits and worldly waves whose
          ebb and flow
Of seafaring traffic is mirrored and reflected in the big screen of
          many a window

And glassy wall of waterside office buildings, all reproducing
So many different seafaring images, scenes and portraits,
          projecting

Them like pop art and an extra-curricular maritime consciousness
          in reflections
Along seaport streets with their fleetingly graphic projections

All shimmering in the hot, hot, sun.
Fleeing images on the run, run, run!

(Catch me some revealing imagery,
Like butterflies, in this glass menagerie.)

And then there are wooden trams, painted green, clattering their
          chattering way
From one end of this intriguing town to the other, each and
          every day

Through a maze of back streets, side streets and Chinese antique
Markets in a riveting scene of deepening fascination that is so
          unique.

And at night when the sky is ablaze with multi-coloured neon
          lights

That change from blue to green to yellow, red, purple and pink
      in flights

Of inevitable fancy, one can visit hotel bars with spacious
      windows overlooking
A different harbour now with its neon dusted and streaked sky
      where so much is cooking

In a rich rainbow stew of colour and stars lighting up the
      darkness. Such magic
And enchantment after dark in which there is a different kind of
      traffic.

And at Yuletide, one million light bulbs shine on neon Santas
      and Reindeers
Where seasonal greetings are painted right across another night
      sky that smears

Its colours high above the seaport, with Christmas carol music
      heard far and wide
Through the exotic streets around that ubiquitous and famous
      waterside.

But some of the most absorbing views of all are those shrouded
      by mist
Which, when it falls, comes down like a massive curtain to
      quickly enlist

A mystery and magic all its own
That is so eerily home grown
Out of this harbour and surrounding seas
In which clear visibility panics and flees.

Here is a lofty poetic mist that is taller than ships and buildings
As it comes in from the sea, as it has done from the beginnings

Of time, this mist sublime
Rolling over the brine.

And when the typhoons come, uprooting trees and ships,
Tossing road vehicles through the air and causing landslips,

We are reminded of what exactly is meant by a great wind
In which so much of the universe can be flattened and binned.

(Great wind is what the word typhoon means in Chinese
And it is so great that it brings this part of the world to its knees).

Some people call this place the New York of the Far East,
But for me it is a movable feast

That is so very much more than that.
Europe in China and China in Europe is where it's at,

Thanks to the English who put it on the world map
In 1842, slap bang in mainland China's fortunate lap,

With a little help from their diligent Cantonese friends
On whom the future of this seaport city still depends.

Of course, this magnetic destination has seen its dog days, but
      they would seem
To be long gone now (there are always such days, wherever one
      has been).

As you will have gathered from this song,
The place of which I speak is Hong Kong.

*Bob Crew*

## CASABIANCA

The boy stood on the burning deck,
    Whence all but him had fled;
The flame that lit the battle's wreck
    Shone round him o'er the dead.

Yet beautiful and bright he stood,
    As born to rule the storm;
A creature of heroic blood,
    A proud though childlike form.

. . .

He called aloud, 'Say, Father, say
    If yet my task be done?'
He knew not that the chieftain lay
    Unconscious of his son.

'Speak, father!' once again he cried,
    'If I may yet be gone!'
And but the booming shots replied,
    And fast the flames rolled on.

Upon his brow he felt their breath,
    And in his waving hair,
And looked from the lone post of death
    In still yet brave despair.

And shouted but once more aloud,
    'My father! must I stay?'
While o'er him fast, through sail and shroud,
    The wreathing fires made way.

They wrapt the ship in splendor wild,
    They caught the flag on high,
And streamed above the gallant child,
    Like banners in the sky.

There came a burst of thunder sound;
    The boy – oh! where was he?
Ask of the winds that far around
    With fragments strewed the sea! –

With shroud and mast, and pennon fair,
    That well had borne their part, –
But the noblest thing which perished there
    Was that young faithful heart.

*Felicia Hemans*

## SEAFARING AND GOLD

Up in the beautiful highlands of the cosmopolitan city of
    Johannesburg,
Not all that far from the breath-taking scenic mountains
    of the Drakensburg,

The world's largest deposits of gold
Have been bought and sold.

This glittering gold – and diamonds too – put a mystical spell on
    the island race,
Which soon sent fleets of many adventurous ships to make
    unrelenting haste

To South Africa, in seafaring days of old,
Carrying gold-mining settlers and soldiers bold.

Spanish galleon gold had nothing on this.
No more high-spirited hit and miss
Acts of fearless and notorious piracy
For dare devil English buccaneers at sea.

This really was big-time diamonds and serious gold
On which the English intended to have a stranglehold.

They established a nineteenth century Colony in the Cape
Where there is a truly magnificent seascape

Known as Cape Town at the foot of Table Mountain, to this day,
So lovely to behold like a glittering jewel in Table Bay.

It was with the colossal wealth from this gold that the English
      statesman,
Cecil Rhodes, emerged on the world scene, with his spectacular
      plan
To build Bechuanaland and also Rhodesia that was named after
      him.
He it was who rose above the tumult and accusative din

Of the Boer War, to make his name
And himself perfectly plain.

He established 170 Rhodes scholarships at England's Oxford
      University
For students from the British Empire, the USA and Germany,

And he lived a life of luxury in what is now Cape Town's
      botanical gardens,
Known as the Kirstenbosch. His was an exciting life that took off
      where the sea ends

And the land begins and begins. But it is out of the sea
That has come all this magnificent history
With gold and diamonds to be found
And dug out of Africa's ground.

In Johannesburg today live Sean and Karen with their baby son,
In an exciting and futuristic country that was by ancient
      seafaring begun.

Go there if you can, you will not regret it,
And you are not very likely to forget it.

*Bob Crew*

# VOYAGING IN

I t appears that there are fewer voyaging-in poems than there are those that voyage out and in between, and perhaps this is because it is more complicated and difficult voyaging into the depths of one's own soul and inner being and making a success of it. One has to dig deeper into one's imagination to describe how one feels and thinks, rather than observing or describing what one sees externally at sea and feels about that – describing is not 100% imagining. When voyaging out to sea there are things there that tell their own story, that have to be described rather than created from scratch, but when voyaging in one has to create much more of the story for oneself, one has to do more than describe. It's not just a matter of describing how one feels about one's inner feelings. One has to discover them first and then create and structure something meaningful out of them, out of an apparent nothing or a complicated something that is not usually clearly defined.

Voyaging in is arguably a greater challenge and more creative than voyaging out – a greater challenge, not only to write, but also to understand, because the reader is taken on an unfamiliar voyage into the complicated mind of the poet, and not just out to the more familiar territory of the sea. Voyaging in explores one's inner thoughts and being, using the sea as an image or metaphor for preoccupations and concerns other than the sea, so it is much more introspective and concerned with self, as are Emily Dickinson's voyaging-in poems in the *From America* section of this book (of course, most poems are concerned with self, but the voyaging-in variety are more self-centred and ego-centric than others).

In the following sample there are five sea poems that are concerned with morality, religion, philosophy, poetry and life, dipping into the sea for their imagery. Some of these poems don't go to sea at all, but stay on dry land to use its imagery from a distance, whilst other poems do take to the ocean waves, but only to voyage into the poet's inner self when they get there.

In 'Dover beach' (1867), for example – by the nineteenth-century English poet Matthew Arnold – there is a strong religious dimension, in which the poet's inner thoughts about the break-down of civilisation and his inner feelings about the turbid ebb and flow of human misery are expressed in terms of sea imagery, and they suggest that the poet and/or narrator may not be able to live without a system of beliefs that recognises the limitations of philosophy in relation to pure faith. Matthew Arnold was the precursor of virtually everything that the Anglo-American poet T. S. Eliot came to stand for in the first part of the twentieth century. I was in two minds about whether to include Arnold's poem in this *Voyaging-in* section, rather than in *Voyaging in between*, but on balance I think that he does voyage in rather more than he voyages out or in between, and that his relation-ship with the sea is much more intellectual and spiritual (from within himself) than it is outwardly emotional or physical. There seems to be a 'closure' in this poem that voyages in, even when the poet is out there (in his imagination and/or in person) on the beach looking at the sea, or looking at it through the window of his house, whilst he is talking about something else entirely. Although the poem begins with outward-bound poetry that is brilliantly descriptive and tenderly poetic, the mood and direction changes when the sea brings its 'eternal note of sadness in', and the narrator does a U-turn. And, whilst 'the sea is calm tonight', it is a calm reflection of one's inner thoughts – 'we find also in the sound a thought' – that we are getting here, with Matthew Arnold voyaging in rather than out.

There is also a twenty-first-century poem, 'Fishing for waves' (2004), in which the poet voyages within his own subconscious and stays there for quite some time, as he digs deep into his imagination, while borrowing imagery from the sea to talk about poetry and life every bit as much as, if not more than, the sea itself. And in Coleridge's 'Rime of the ancient mariner' (1798), the poet goes into his own imagination and inner thoughts to conjure up a fictional or fictionalised morality tale in which there is a supernatural punishment and penance for a seaman who has heartlessly and without conscience or any moral awareness shot a precious albatross, in a narrative that is told by the Ancient Mariner to a listener who is on his way to a wedding (this is a long ballad poem, of which only an excerpt is included here).

We also have an excerpt from D. H. Lawrence's twentieth-century 'The ship of death' (1917) that takes us on a ship, not to voyage out to sea, but to voyage instead into the poet's land-based inner thoughts about death, on the last journey of all. And, in 'A splash of poetry' (2005), we have a short poem about life and death told in terms of the sea.

Hopefully, there is a nice balance in this section of poems spanning four different centuries, each with different examples of the same voyaging-in process, revealing how poets voyage into themselves without, if they are lucky, getting lost at sea within themselves – whilst also demonstrating how the psychological dynamic between seafaring and the writing of poetry works.

## DOVER BEACH

The sea is calm tonight.
The tide is full, the moon lies fair
Upon the straits; – on the French coast the light
Gleams and is gone; the cliffs of England stand,
Glimmering and vast, out in the tranquil bay.
Come to the window, sweet is the night-air!
Only, from the long line of spray
Where the sea meets the moon-blanch'd sand,
Listen! You hear the grating roar
Of pebbles which the waves draw back, and fling,
And their return, up the high strand,
Begin, and cease, and then again begin,
With tremulous cadence slow, and bring
The eternal note of sadness in.

Sophocles long ago
Heard it on the Aegean, and it brought
Into his mind the turbid ebb and flow
Of human misery; we
Find also in the sound a thought,
Hearing it by this distant northern sea.

The sea of faith
Was once, too, at the full, and round earth's shore
Lay like the folds of a bright girdle furl'd.
But now I only hear
Its melancholy, long, withdrawing roar,
Retreating, to the breath
Of the night-winds, down the vast edges drear
And naked shingles of the world.

Ah, love, let us be true
To one another! for the world, which seems
To lie before us like a land of dreams,
So various, so beautiful, so new,
Hath really neither joy, nor love, nor light,
Nor certitude, nor peace, nor help for pain;
And we are here as on a darkling plain
Swept with confus'd alarms of struggle and flight,
Where ignorant armies clash by night.

*Matthew Arnold*

## FISHING FOR WAVES

There are more waves
Than there are fish in the sea,
But it's impossible to catch one
With the widest net
Or at the end of the longest rod

And that's because the sea behaves,
Like the poet, mysteriously,
In the ebb and flow of language and song
That is so salty and dripping wet
With imagery, in need of a helpful nod
From the Neptune or Poseidon God.

But what is a fast-running wave other than poetry?
Fast-flowing poetry read at a rapid rate that is
an everywhere of silver, an underwear of green,
an over there of blue, an over here of white,
an in and out of yellowy green as a bean,
a topsy curvy-turvy of pea soup, a spilt pot of paint,
a canvas of waves, a parchment of paper, a trembling excitement,
a drenched and watery rainbow streaming with colour, the
colour of your soul, a sea-train racing along the ocean's track, an
up and down of the sea's gown, a flash of sky – or was it thigh? –
a fluid image of fleeting mermaid, slippery as a fish, a silvery
catch-me-if-you-can fish, a sea-saw jigsaw of the sea, a slippery
slope of waves, a helter skelter of mermaids, a wavy ice-rink of
sea, dead in the water waves, belly up waves, waves that stand
up and fight, shaking their fists, a deep and horrifying debt of
waves, doom and gloom waves, waves of dismay and sadness –
a tristesse of waves – Kitty Witch waves, call of the curlew
waves, a grave of waves, high-interest waves, payback waves,
waves that smile and laugh like flowers waving from a distance,
waves of deep relaxation, meditation and healing, a perfumed
garden of waves, sea-breeze waves that touch a nerve and unfold
a sail, the sail of the mind, waves that visit the respective shores

of the sub-conscious and unconscious minds – a rich vein of
waves to be mined like silver, gold and diamond mines – a
reverie of waves with which to imagine and to explore amazing
things, an astonishment of waves, altered images and states of
consciousness, waves to find the motor in the brain and break all
the speed limits, spinning-top waves, a dream and scream of
waves, a shell of waves and a wave of shells, shells painted on a
wallpaper of waves, free-flowing waves,  a freedom of waves, a
blindness of waves, shift of wind waves, waves of every
conceivable image, a plumage of waves, a rich language of waves
on which to get high, a tongue twister of waves, sprung-rhythm
waves right across the senses – with spring in their step as they
go down that royal road to the sub-conscious and unconscious
mind that is such a sea of resources just waiting to be utilised,
high road and low road waves, fast track and slow track – waves
as tall as a tall ship and as small as  a sea urchin, tall-story waves,
stretch-limo waves to stretch all credibility, waves you can and
cannot trust, a leafy carpet of waves, a low-lying cloud of waves
and of poetry, waves writing poetry in the sea, a distant mountain range, a roller coaster, deep ravines, canyons and valleys, a
dark forest of waves, a steamy landfall and earthquake of waves,
a plague of wild and wavy places, a swarm of waves, waves from
hell, a marshy swampland of waves, sea of misery waves, waves
of washed away wishes, cyclone alleys and back streets and high
roads of waves, a sniff and inhalation of waves, waves to chill the
spine of the universe, waves to break your heart, a sea of mess,
soulful and soul-searching waves, waves with double-meanings,
an hysteria of waves, waves jumping out of their skins, ships and
sailors jumping out of theirs, shrinking and sinking ships,
shrinking and sinking souls, waves shrinking from the cold and
from other waves, thunderous waves shrinking from nothing,
shrinking and sinking sea mists, waves of hope and despair,
waves to sink your soul – a giddy frenzy of waves, mist, thunder
and cloud – a throng and song of waves, busy waves, neap and
lazy waves, sleeping waves, sweet-dream waves, wet dream
waves, sleeping dog waves that bark like seals when disturbed,
monstrous waves, monsters with fanged teeth, a snake pit of a

sea full of serpents – a slithering snake of waves plundering
their way down the rippling page of the sea as it pervades our
consciousness, signalling movement and visual impact as it coils
round our inner-thoughts – buccaneering waves plundering
images like pirates, a gathering dust and lust of waves, a creeping sea mist sneaking into our minds, a glimmer and shimmer of
waves – a tall smoky chimney of waves, a tangle of waves, a sea
of crime, virtue and bravery, morality and immorality – a sea of
deeds and shared intentions, an unbroken silence, a tight-lipped
sea, waves that mix and un-mix their metaphors – a bulldozer
and concrete mixer of a sea, a splish-splash of mist and an ele-
gant tracery of spray, a grasshopper reflection, a blade of grassy
sea, a curved shape with no form, an undertone of waves, waves
hooked like fish, waves dissolving like cubes of sugar in a cup of
hot coffee (or is it tea?), a rough trade of waves, a madness of
waves, a mighty fragile force destined to burst like a bubble,
bursting with so much light and colour – a darting brush stroke,
swift impressions of the sea – fast brush strokes in search of an
essence of fleeting truth, belief and disbelief, an intelligent dis-
cussion in the eye of the storm, an imagined sea that comes out
of the fanciful imagination of poetry, a key with which to
unlock the mystery of the sea and of poetry, a sea that minds its
own business and keeps its own conscience, a colourful sea in
the eyes of the world, a sea that puts everything into context and
then takes it out again, a confusing and contradictory sea bursting with the dynamic dualism of life – the good and the bad, the
constructive and destructive – an intellectually and physically
exhausting sea, a picture that refuses to sink, a spray of paint,
tinctures of water colour from the rivers of the world, a watery
pasture, a haystack of waves, a seasonal mixture of colour, an egg
white and bleach of snow, a cracking and breaking of glass, a
breaking and smashing of waves, a crushing of ice, a growling
volcano under an upside down mountain of ice that threatens to
burst into black clouds, a lick of fiery waves, a streak of streaky
lightning, a pigment of fog, waves bathed in moonlight and shot
through with glinting ice, a precious gleam of dream-light and
moonlight, a presence and absence of sunlight, a rainfall of

starlight, a twinkle of distant lights, a shower of spray, vision of summer sunlight, cold of cold wintry light, gloom of gloom and dark of dark, so many transient moods and moments lit up by light, the sea filtered through light, images within images, waves within waves, the riddle of tidal sands with their pulsating undercurrents of consciousness, translucence of crystal-clear blue under the sun, electric blue, an oasis of beauty under the sea, waves beneath clouds writing poetry in the sky, waves that write the story for you, a journalism and publishing industry of waves, waves to sweep and wash the world away, quickening impressions upon impressions like the quickening spirit in sexual union, a thrusting and tempestuous seabed with the legs of mother sea wide apart, open and welcoming, a hostile bed with her legs tightly crossed, a heaving bosom and swelling breast of waves, a ripple and nipple of waves, a rapture of waves, waves as curvaceous as a woman's body, naked and erotic waves, voluptuous waves, waves of creative resource, speed-painting waves, an osmosis of ocean from fluid waves to fluid thoughts, a precarious heap of toppling waves, a chaos and mirror of waves, blizzards teaming with snowflakes and hailstones, lighthouses lanterning the pitch-black dark, orangey hazy-light creeping and trickling through the amber-splashed dark, a wash of rain, a candyfloss of blue and green, emerald and turquoise, sunset bronze and gold, silver and purple, and daily-grey of grey, a pot of sea-weedy paint, salty paint, a world globed in blue, a torrent of reflections, a shattered remnant, a shadow in the sea, a weeping wind, tears from heaven, tears of blood, a floating tapestry, forgotten history, a sea and fountain of thought – maybe even faith – thought floating or flying and crying like a seagull, a melancholy of purple loneliness, a darting image, a shoal of illusions and hallucinations, a churned up and foamy slice of icing-sugar magic, a slice of wave, a tidal mirage, a grain of blue sand in a swampy desert of rising and falling dunes, for which time is running out, the wet and slippery briny-sands of time, a storm of sand, an echo in a cave, in the echoing caves of the mind to remind us all that a racing ducking-and-diving wave, like life itself, rushing and gushing, is transient, impermanent, monstrously fragile but will sink us in the end, to remind us all that it is impossible to have or to hold, to catch or to keep. So – phew! wow! – rest your restless head, don't lose sleep, don't fret, or forget that it's not worth it. You can never catch an elusive exploding wave – so fish instead for poetry, waves and oceans of poetry, let them wash over you and sweep you away – because a wave is a ghostly spirit from the ocean – a phantom, a genie out of a floating gloating bottle – a slippery, slippery, slippery, echo.... echo ... echo ... a breathless whisper, all this and more lost at sea until the poet brings it ashore like a message in a bottle, an endlessly long and sweeping drifting-and-swelling sentence with no beginning and no end ... the longest flow of image, vision and metaphor in the world with which to steal the show ... an interrupted thought and wash of poetry with no end ...

*Bob Crew*

## THE RIME OF THE ANCIENT MARINER
### (*an excerpt*)

'At length did cross an albatross –
Through the fog it came:
As if it had been a Christian soul,
We hailed it in God's name.

'It ate the food it ne'er had eat,
And round and round it flew:
The ice did split, with a thunder-fit;
The helmsman steered us through!

'And a good south wind sprung up behind, –
The albatross did follow,
And every day, for food or play,
Came to the mariners' hollo.

'In mist or cloud, on mast or shroud,
It perched for vespers nine;
While all the night, through fog-smoke white,
Glimmered the white moonshine.'

'God save thee, ancient Mariner,
From the fiends that plague thee thus! –
Why look'st thou so?' – 'With my crossbow
I shot the Albatross.'

———

'And I had done a hellish thing,
And it would work 'em woe;
For all averr'd, I had killed the bird
That made the breeze to blow.
"Ah, wretch!" said they, "the bird to slay,
That made the breeze to blow!"

———

'The fair breeze blew, the white foam flew;
The furrow followed free:
We were the first that ever burst
Into that silent sea!

'Down dropt the breeze; the sails dropt down, -
'Twas sad as sad could be;
And we did speak only to break
The silence of the sea.

'All in a hot and copper sky
The bloody sun, at noon,
Right above the mast did stand,
No bigger than the moon.

'Day after day, day after day
We stuck – nor breath nor motion –
As idle as a painted ship
Upon a painted ocean!

'Water, water, everywhere –
And all the boards did shrink!
Water, water, everywhere,
Nor any drop to drink!

*Samuel Taylor Coleridge*

## THE SHIP OF DEATH
### (*an excerpt*)

Have you built your ship of death, O have you?
O build your ship of death, for you will need it.

The grim frost is at hand, when the apples will fall
thick, almost thundrous, on the hardened earth.

And death is on the air like a smell of ashes!
Ah! can't you smell it?

And in the bruised body, the frightened soul
finds itself shrinking, wincing from the cold
that blows upon it through the orifices.

*D. H. Lawrence*


## A SPLASH OF POETRY

A single drop of water between narrow banks in the drip
     and  slip of time.
A droplet, a trickle and a ripple at the crack and smack of
     dawn with its lifeline.
A stream, a river bursting its banks, an ooze, a flood and an
     estuary.
A splash in the sea, a sinking ship, a wreckage and a splash
     of poetry.
A deep ocean's bottom
Where all is forgotten.

*Bob Crew*

# *VOYAGING IN BETWEEN*

B etween the poetry that voyages out (onto the ocean waves to describe life at sea and tell of its seafarers, stories, myths and mysteries), and the poetry that voyages in (deep into a poet's inner self, as he or she borrows the imagery of the sea to tell about things other than the sea, or to seriously examine one's inner feelings), there is the in-between poetry, which doesn't quite do one or the other of these things, because it is exiled from them both – exiled from the sea beyond the shores that surround us, and from most of the sea within us. Voyaging neither in nor out, this is a poetry that talks or expresses sentiments about the sea, or about voyaging out one day, without actually going there, and it refers to things about the inner self without exploring them in any real depth, or nakedly revealing them, with any seriously introspective soul-searching, such as we see in Emily Dickinson's poetry. We are talking in this section about the kind of poetry that doesn't commit either way, as it shows how people and poets relate to the oceans of the world, without actually being on them, or to sea battles that are described from the shore, basing their poems on them, as they steer a course in between the sea within themselves and the sea offshore.

This in-between poetry usually relates to the sea from a cliff top, a beach, the course of a river, or somewhere inland, looking abroad, across the sea from a distance, or talking about the sea from the shore, without going to sea and getting wet (unless paddling) or getting deep into the subject of the sea, as the poem splashes around, ankle deep, between both worlds. This can be the poetry of longing that longs for the sea and/or the outside world without becoming part of it. It can also be the poetry that warns against the sea.

In this section we see how such poems use the imagery of the sea either to express sexual longing, or simply a longing for the sea itself (if not a mixture of the two), or to make a comment about life and people on land, if not about the sea itself, events at sea, or about poetry. There are poems here about dead bodies that are washed up on the shore from the sea, and about battles fought at sea.

There is also poetry here that comments very specifically on the destructive nature of the sea, as well as its therapeutic nature, and there is a poem in which the poet likens himself to the sea, and another in which Shakespeare's genius is likened to the sea. This in-between poetry borrows from the sea, to make a comparison with it, or to talk about it or about something else entirely, but without embarking on a proper journey, and it shows how the sea makes itself felt to those who are not actually voyaging one way or the other, but observing or thinking about the sea nevertheless.

This is the kind of poetry that can never get the irresistible sea or seafarers out of its mind, but which can never give itself over entirely to a proper sea poem, or inner-self poem. If the sea or the inner self is not the objective of the poem, then it obviously has no need to voyage out or in. At the same time, the poem remains enthralled by, or aware of the sea, just as voyaging-out and voyaging-in poems do.

## A WILD AND STORMY SEA
## BRINGS OUT THE WILDNESS IN ME

She said: I want to get out of the car and walk along this dark cliff-top with the wind in my hair and the rain beating on my face.

He said: It's a gale-force wind out there, you will have to *stride* along the cliff-top and we'll soon be soaked to the skin in this wet and stormy place.

She said: I don't care. I'd like that.

He thought: So that's where she's at.

She said: I want to hear the waves crashing against the rocks and pounding the shore down there.

He thought: She has other rocks in mind, but what do I care?

She said: I want to be wind-lashed and wet all over.

He said: It's too cold to go naked and roll in the clover.

She said: A wild and stormy sea
brings out the wildness in me.
It puts me in a wild mood.

He said: You like to live dangerously
and that's one hell of a thought on which to brood.

She said: Wait and see.

He said: Always the patient one, that's me.

She said:    I want your hot rod to crash and splash into me,
like a mighty wave, hurling and pouring its
foaming passion right into the depth of me, like the
angry, storm-tossed sea. I want you to do it to me
like the sea, up against this cold cliff, before we go.

He said:    I know.

She said:    I want to be sucked in and swallowed up by your
deepest undercurrents, swept away by the ebb and
flow of your fast-flowing waves. I want to feel the
throb and tug of you, the mighty swell of you, as
you pound me. But first we'll get soaked in the
rain, striding along this cliff in the dark.

He thought:  What a lark.
She wants me to nail her and sail her.

*Bob Crew*

SEA LOVE

Tide be runnin' the great world over:
    'Twas only last June month I mind that we
Was thinkin' the toss and the call in the breast of the lover
    So everlastin' as the sea.

Heer's the same little fishes that sputter and swim,
    Wi' the moon's old glim on the grey, wet sand;
An' him no more to me nor me to him
    Than the wind goin' over my hand.

*Charlotte Mew*

## SEAMAN 1941
### (*an excerpt*)

This was not to be expected.

Waves, wind, and tide brought him again
to Barra. Clinging to driftwood many hours
the night before, he had not recognized
the current far offshore his own nor
known he drifted home. He gave up, anyway,
some time before the smell of land reached out
or dawn outlined the morning gulls.

They found him
on the white sand southward of the ness,
not long enough in the sea to be
disfigured, cheek sideways as in sleep,
old men who had fished with his father
and grandfather and knew him at once,
before they even turned him on his back, by the set
of the dead shoulders, and were shocked.

This was not to be expected.

His mother, with hot eyes, preparing the parlour
for his corpse, would have preferred, she thought,
to have been told by telegram rather
than so to know that convoy, ship, and son
had only been a hundred miles north-west
of home when the torpedoes struck.

*Molly Holden*

## THE BOY STOOD ON THE BURNING DECK

Tell me, Felicia, what happened to the charred remains
Of that poor disastrous boy who went up in flames?

When he was tragically no more
Did his blistered corpse float in to shore?

Was he washed away by a sea
Indifferent to his fiery agony?

Or did the cool lick of the sea soothe the hot wounds
 of this brave little lad
Who repeatedly called out in vain for his dad?

What a kingsize drama – titanic in more ways than one –
There is to be found in the sea when all is said and done.

How can we ever forget the boy who stood on the burning deck
When those about him quickly fled?

This boy for whom so many hearts bled
After his ship became a war-torn wreck.

*Bob Crew*

## THE ARMADA
*(an excerpt)*

Attend, all ye who list to hear our noble England's praise;
I tell of the thrice famous deeds she wrought in ancient days,
When that great fleet invincible against her bore in vain
The richest spoils of Mexico, the stoutest hearts of Spain.

It was about the lovely close of a warm summer day,
There came a gallant merchant-ship full sail to Plymouth Bay;
Her crew hath seen Castile's black fleet, beyond Aurigny's isle,
At earliest twilight, on the waves lie heaving many a mile.
At sunrise she escaped their van, by God's especial grace;
And the tall Pinta, till the noon, had held her close in chase.
Forthwith a guard at every gun was placed along the wall;
The beacon blazed upon the roof of Edgecumbe's lofty hall;
Many a light fishing-bark put out to pry along the coast,
And with loose rein and bloody spur rode inland many a post.
With his white hair unbonneted, the stout old sheriff comes;
Behind him march the halberdiers; before him sound the drums;
His yeomen round the market cross make clear an ample space;
For there behoves him to set up the standard of Her Grace.
And haughtily the trumpets peal, and gaily dance the bells,
As slow upon the labouring wind the royal blazon swells.
Look how the Lion of the sea lifts up his ancient crown,
And underneath his deadly paw treads the gay lilies down.
So stalked he when he turned to flight, on that famed Picard field,
Bohemia's plume, and Genoa's bow, and Caesar's eagle shield.
So glared he when at Agincourt in wrath he turned to bay,
And crushed and torn beneath his claws the princely hunters lay.
Ho! Strike the flagstaff deep, Sir Knight: ho! Scatter flowers, fair
        maids:
Ho! gunners, fire a loud salute: ho! gallants, draw your blades:

Thou sun, shine on her joyously; ye breezes, waft her wide;
Our glorious SEMPER EADEM, the banner of our pride.
The freshening breeze of eve unfurled that banner's massy fold;
The parting gleam of sunshine kissed that haughty scroll of gold;
Night sank upon the dusky beach, and on the purple sea,
Such night in England ne'er had been, nor ne'er again shall be.

*Thomas Babington Macaulay*

## BY THE SEA

Why does the sea moan evermore?
    Shut out from heaven it makes its moan,
It frets against the boundary shore;
    All earth's full rivers cannot fill
    The sea, that drinking thirsteth still.

Sheer miracles of loveliness
    Lie hid in its unlooked-on bed:
Anemones, salt, passionless,
    Blow flower-like; just enough alive
    To blow and multiply and thrive.

Shells quaint with curve, or spot, or spike,
    Encrusted live things argus-eyed,
All fair alike, yet all unlike,
    Are born without a pang, and die
    Without a pang, and so pass by.

*Christina Rossetti*

## A METAPHOR FOR LIFE

What a garden for flowering poetry
The sea has made for us on a good day.

Such a lily pond for fine thoughts
And a lake for calm reflections.

But, on a bad day, what a nasty stew of turmoil and cold bleak
       misery,
Such a ferocious and dangerous enemy to be shored up and kept
       at bay
When the wicked wintry elements are wildly out of sorts,
Swamping and sinking us with nature's implacable rejections.

What a ceaseless flood of fanciful foam
On which to let our thoughts race and roam.

So many swimming, swarming images and ideas, rising up out
       of the sea,
Shaking off their wet leaves like fine spray from an Atlantis tree.

What a warm summer of love
When the heavens above
Are shining and smiling
And the distant shores are so beguiling,
Beckoning us over the shimmering horizon.

Such a source of beauty and wonder
In the great blue yonder.

What a wonderful opiate for mankind to be on
Until there is a glowering change of climate and mood,
When we are suddenly left with such indigestible food
For alternative thought, as we choke on our words and quickly
       find

A cruel and savage sea of a woefully different and less friendly
      kind!

Such a metaphor for life as we attempt to read the sea
And its contradictory pages of unfathomable mystery.

*Bob Crew*


## FROM EYE TO EYE

One cannot go to sea
Without knowing the dark
And terrible forces of the universe.

One can never ever be
Unaware of this stark
Reality that is the reverse

Of Emerson's gorgeous sail.
One cannot fail
To know how spurious

Is gorgeous
When the mood changes
And the universe rages

From sky to sky
And eye to eye.

Down the long road of the bold
Until the seafarer's story is finally told.

*Bob Crew*

## ON THE SEA

It keeps eternal whisperings around
    Desolate shores, and with its mighty swell
    Gluts twice ten thousand caverns, till the spell
Of  Hecate leaves them their old shadowy sound.
Often 'tis in such gentle temper found,
    That scarcely will the very smallest shell
    Be moved for days from whence it sometime fell,
When last the winds of heaven were unbound.
Oh ye! who have your eye-balls vexed and tired,
    Feast them upon the wideness of the Sea;
Oh ye! whose ears are dinned with uproar rude,
Or fed too much with cloying melody, –
    Sit ye near some old cavern's mouth, and brood
Until ye start, as if the sea-nymphs quired!

               *John Keats*

## MANA OF THE SEA

Do you see the sea, breaking itself to bits against
    the islands
yet remaining unbroken, the level great sea?

Have I caught from it
the tide in my arms
that runs down to the shallows of my wrists,
    and breaks
abroad in my hands, like waves among the rocks
    of substance?

Do the rollers of the sea
roll down my thighs
and over the submerged islets of my knees
with power, sea-power
sea-power
to break against the ground
in the flat, recurrent breakers of my two feet?

And is my body ocean, ocean
whose power runs to the shores along my arms
and breaks in the foamy hands, whose power rolls out
to the white-treading waves of two salt feet?

I am the sea, I am the sea!

*D. H. Lawrence*

## DIAPASON

You know the rocks and shallows
You warn
You show the narrow channel
The safe harbour
Sound out in the mist,
Make your voice heard

Raise your voice, poet,
Your warning sound
This is no clear day
When you can sleep

*Martin Eve*

## DOVER CLIFFS

On these white cliffs, that calm above the flood
Uplift their shadowy heads, and at their feet
Scarce hear the surge that has for ages beat,
Sure many a lonely wanderer has stood;
And whilst the lifted murmur met his ear,
And o'er the distant billows the still eve
Sailed slow, has thought of all his heart must leave
Tomorrow; of the friends he loved most dear;
Of social scenes from which he wept to part.
But if, like me, he knew how fruitless all
The thoughts that would full fain the past recall;
Soon would he quell the risings of his heart,
And brave the wild winds and unhearing tide,
The world his country, and his God his guide.

*William Lisle Bowles*

## WHEN THE SEA STRIKES BACK

Aided by global warming
The angry sea is preparing to rise up
Like a giant monster and strike back,
To rise high above the sinking land
Where it will soon show its shadowy hand
And without too much warning,
As waves, like shock troops, overspill its cup
And go on the attack.

Towering tidally above the slipping-sliding land
And its surrounding helter-skelter pebble and sand
In a final cliff hanging and toppling push
That will swiftly gush and rush
Into every falling town and city,
The unstoppable sea will carry all before it and show no mercy
As it swamps our washed-out world and sweeps it away forever,
Swallowing it up in a deepening gloom, as if the world had
         never
Before existed on the puzzled face of the earth,
Or had any conceivable purpose or worth
In nature's precious plan
And the sea's mighty span.

Aided by *atrocious* global warming,
And already made redundant by the aeroplane,
The resentful sea will be massively unforgiving
As we all become swiftly and completely insane
With ferocious drowning, drowning, drowning,
While the oceans are spitefully gloating and frowning
At our devastated world, as it recedes into a future
In which it is painted into a seascape of a swirling-whirling
         picture,

With a rapidly sinking globe that is sucked down the
      horrifying drain
Of the deadly deep, like a tragic lead-balloon, because
      man forgot to use his brain
That is supposed to be so much deeper than the sea
(But how can that be, sweet Emily?).

Airports will sink in the swelling, smirking sea,
As will cars, motorways, houses and buildings,
Until the oceans of revenge are able to roam free,
Perhaps floating some new beginnings
Here and there, when we are no more
Because we are anchored to the dark floor
Of the sea,
Shamed by our history.
Believe me,

The sea will have the last laugh –
A rasping laugh and a half!
It will be good riddance to us.
No fuss!

*Bob Crew*

## ROLL ON, THOU DEEP AND DARK BLUE OCEAN
### (*an excerpt from Childe Harold's Pilgrimage*)

Roll on, thou deep and dark blue Ocean – roll!
Ten thousand fleets sweep over thee in vain;
Man marks the earth with ruin – his control
Stops with the shore; – upon the watery plain
The wrecks are all thy deed, nor doth remain
A shadow of man's ravage, save his own,
When, for a moment, like a drop of rain,
He sinks into thy depths with bubbling groan,
Without a grave, unknell'd, uncoffin'd, and unknown.

*George Gordon, Lord Byron*

## SHAKESPEARE'S EYE IN THE STORM

I have sometimes heard it said
That the actress, Vivien Leigh,
Who to Sir Laurence Olivier was wed,
Has compared Shakespeare to the sea,
Saying that we can swim around in his genius
And go where we like, letting it wash all over us.

And her husband,
Who had a hand
In many a Shakespeare play,
Has also had his say,
Likening the bard's drama and poetry,
Not just to the interminable sea,
But to an incarnation, no less,
Of the eye of God. Goodness
Gracious me!
I think I prefer the sea.

But it is good to think of Britain afloat in a sea of poetry
And the world's best theatre for all to enjoy and to see,
Encircled offshore by a keenly observant, all-seeing eye,
Under a glowering and/or smiling contradictory sky.
An eye in the storm that shines out like a lighthouse
        beacon
To keep our civilisation afloat and give us much indeed
        to think on.

*Bob Crew*

## FULL FATHOM FIVE
### (*from* The Tempest)

Full fathom five thy father lies;
 Of his bones are coral made;
Those are pearls that were his eyes;
 Nothing of him that doth fade,
But doth suffer a sea-change
Into something rich and strange.
Sea-nymphs hourly ring his knell:
 Ding-dong.
Hark! Now I hear them –
 Ding-dong, bell!

*William Shakespeare*

## THE LANDING OF THE PILGRIM FATHERS
## IN NEW ENGLAND

Look now abroad – another race has fill'd
Those populous borders – wide the wood recedes,
And town shoots up, and fertile realms are till'd
The land is full of harvest and green meads.

The breaking waves dash'd high
On a stern and rock-bound coast,
And the woods against a stormy sky
Their giant branches toss'd;

And the heavy night hung dark,
The hills and water o'er,
When a band of exiles moor'd their bark
On the wild New England shore.

Not as the conqueror comes,
They, the true hearted, came;
Not with the roll of the stirring drums,
And the trumpet that sings of fame;

Not as the flying come,
In silence and in fear; –
They shook the depths of the desert gloom
With their hymns of lofty cheer.

Amidst the storm they sang,
And the stars heard and the sea:
And the sounding aisles of the dim woods rang
To the anthem of the free!

The ocean eagle soar'd
From his nest by the white wave's foam
And the rocking pines of the forest roar'd –
This was their welcome home!

There were men with hoary hair
Amidst that pilgrim band; –
Why had they come to wither there,
Away from their childhood's land?

There was woman's fearless eye,
Lit by her deep love's truth;
There was manhood's brow serenely high,
And the fiery heart of youth.

What sought they thus afar?
Bright jewels of the mine?
The wealth of seas, the spoils of war? –
They sought a faith's pure shrine!

Ay, call it holy ground,
The soil where first they trod!
They have left unstain'd what there they found –
Freedom to worship God.

*Felicia Hemans*

## DRAKE

*Excerpts from 'Drake', an early-twentieth-century 498-page marathon
poem about the life and times of the fearless Sir Francis Drake and his
astonishing defeat of the mighty Spanish Armada in 1588, when
Catholic Spain claimed divine authority for its crusade against
Protestant England, and sent 130 ships into the English Channel, complete with an army of soldiers for a planned invasion after the expected
defeat of the English navy, which failed to materialise. This colossus of
an epic poem was originally serialised in Blackwood's Magazine before
being turned into a hardback serial novel. It must be one of the longest
narratives of sea poetry of all time. It is also an historical document of
sorts. The unflappable Drake's cool and calm refusal to fight the
Spanish until he was good and ready, after he had finished a game of
bowls at Plymouth, became the stuff of legend, as he showed the
Spanish the contempt that he obviously thought they richly deserved,
before proceeding to walk rings round them with his (sea) dogs of war.
But, as we see from this poem that corrects history, it wasn't quite like
that, because there were other more serious reasons why this wise and
wily warrior was in no hurry, and quite right too. We also see the
severe plight and hardship of ordinary English seamen – and their
massive contribution to the defeat of the Spanish.*

*In this poem, the poet voyages out but mostly in between to recreate
a sea battle that raged some three centuries previously.*

———

Few minutes, and well wasted those, were spent
On that great game of bowls; for well knew Drake
What panic threatened Plymouth, since his fleet
Lay trapped there by the black head-wind that blew
Straight up the Sound, and Plymouth town itself,
Except the ships won seaward ere the dawn,
Lay at the Armada's mercy. Never a sea-man
Of all the sea-dogs clustered on the quays,
And all the captains clamouring round Lord Howard,
Hoped that one ship might win to the open sea:
At dawn, they thought, the Armada's rolling guns

To windward, in an hour, must shatter them,
Huddled in their red slaughter-house like sheep.

––––––––

Planning to pluck the Armada plume by plume,
Swooped down upon that prey and swiftly engaged
Her desperate guns; while Drake, our ocean-king,
Knowing the full worth of that doom-fraught hour,
Glanced neither to the left nor right, but stood
High on his poop, with calm implacable face
Gazing as into eternity, and steered
The crowded glory of his dawn-flushed sails
In superb onset, straight for the great fleet
Invincible; and after him the main
Of England's fleet, knowing its captain now,
Followed, and with them rushed – from sky to sky
One glittering charge of wrath – the storm's white waves,
The twenty thousand foaming chariots
Of God.

––––––––

Risen from hell, with all the powers of hell
At his command, a face tempered like steel
In the everlasting furnaces, a rock
Of adamant, while with a voice that blent
With the ebb and flow of the everlasting sea
He spake, and at the low deep menacing words
Monotonous with the unconquerable
Passion and level strength of his great soul
They shuddered; for the man seemed more than man,
And from his iron lips resounded doom
As from the lips of cannon, doom to Spain,
Inevitable, unconquerable doom.

––––––––

The fleets were passing Calais and the wind
Blew fair behind them. A strange impulse seized

Spain to shake off those bloodhounds from her trail,
And suddenly the whole Invincible Fleet
Anchored, in hope the following wind would bear
The ships of England past and carry them down
To leeward. But their grim insistent watch
Was ready; and though their van had well-nigh crashed
Into the rear of Spain, in the golden dusk,
They, too, a cannon-shot away, at once
Anchored, to windward still.

———

No more than that great Empire of the deep
Which rolls from Pole to Pole, washing the World
With thunder, that great Empire whose command
This day is yours to take. Hear me, my Queen,
This is a dream, a new dream, but a true;
For mightier days are dawning on the world
Than heart of man hath known. If England hold
The sea, she holds the hundred thousand gates
That open to futurity. She holds
The highway of all ages. Argosies
Of unknown glory set their sails this day
For England out of ports beyond the stars.

———

Across the Atlantic
Great rumours rushed as of a mighty wind,
The wind of the spirit of Drake. But who shall tell
In this cold age the power that he became
Who drew the universe within his soul
And moved with cosmic forces? Though the deep
Divided it from Drake, the gorgeous court
Of Philip shuddered away from the streaming coasts
As a wind-cuffed field of golden wheat. The King,
Bidding his guests to a feast in his own ship
On that wind-darkened sea, was made a mock,
As one by one his ladies proffered excuse

For fear of That beyond. Round Europe now
Ballad and story told how in the cabin
Of Francis Drake there hung a magic glass
Wherein he saw the fleets of all his enemies
And all that passed aboard them.

———

And Spain knows well that flag of fiery fame,
Spain knows who leads those files across the sea;
Implacable, invincible, his name
*El Draque*, creeps hissing through her rank to lee;

———

Her Voice [Queen Elizabeth I] –
    'My people, though my flesh be woman,
My heart is of your kingly lion's breed:
I come myself to lead you!' I see the sun
Shining upon her armour, hear the voice
Of all her armies roaring like one sea –

———

Walsingham stood at his stirrup, muttering 'Ride,
Ride now like hell to Plymouth; for the Queen
Is hard beset, and ere ye are out at sea
Her mood will change. The friends of Spain will move
Earth and the heavens for your recall. They'll tempt her
With their false baits of peace, though I shall stand
Here at your back through thick and thin, farewell!'
Fire flashed beneath the hoofs and Drake was gone.

———

The people
fight
This war of ours, not princes. In this hour
God maketh us a people. We have seen
Victories, never victory like to this,
When in our England's darkest hour of need
Her seamen, without wage, powder, or food,
Are yet on fire to fight for her. Your ships
Tossing in the great sunset of an Empire,
Dawn of a sovereign people, are all manned
By heroes, ragged, hungry, who will die
Like flies ere long, because they have no food
But turns to fever-breeding carrion
Not fit for dogs. They are half-naked, hopeless
Living, of any reward; and if they die
They die a dog's death. We shall reap the fame
While they – great God! and all this cannot quench
The glory in their eyes. They will be served
Six at the mess of four, eking it out
With what their own rude nets may catch by night,
Silvering the guns and naked arms that haul
Under the stars with silver past all price,
While some small ship-boy in the black crow's nest
Watches across the waters for the foe.

*Alfred Noyes*

## SCATTERING HIS ASHES ON THE THAMES

Scattering his ashes on the Thames
Off Waterloo Bridge in Central London
And thinking of how the irresistible call of the sea
Took him to humid Hong Kong where he prematurely
Died of too many cigarettes and an attack of asthma,

I am reminded of how much depends
On our luck in this random life. Oh yes! On
That we can depend. And I know how his three
Young children, predictably in shock, will sorely
Miss their dearly beloved father.

Okay, so some of us make our own luck,
But even so, none of us can ever duck
It altogether. However we may box clever,
We cannot be entirely shot of it. We can never
Be free of luck any more than we can be free
Of the encircling and everywhere sea,
An ocean of bad luck for some,
But not for everyone.

It was the call of the sea that took him by air to polluted Hong
        Kong
When courting his wife to be.
They listened to the tempting song of the ever musical and
        wildly rhythmic sea
Whose music rolls in from the Thames Estuary,
As they looked down the sweeping ocean-bound
River from Waterloo Bridge by the National Theatre, and found
Themselves, before long, in fascinating Hong Kong, as a result
Of pursuing an adventurous thought
Of the inspirational outside world,
By which they were instantly thrilled.

Waterloo Bridge is where they promised each other to go abroad
And see the outside world. And they were as good as their word.
But now that he, at 39, is so prematurely dead,
His ashes are scattered on a watery bed,
Carried by the weeping winds of time
That eternally breeze over the inescapable brine,
Over the River Thames at the centre of the world
Where the city of London is so magnificently curled
Around this mother of all rivers, having sent its ships near and far
In the well-remembered global days of Jolly Jack Tar.

The Mayflower set sail for the New World on the eastern side of
    Tower Bridge,
With the founding fathers of the United States of America, and
    what a privilege
That turned out to be for them, this intrepid band of seafaring
    women and men
In search of a fresh start on a distant shore where they hoped to
    find themselves when
They finally got to their destination, way beyond the National
    Maritime Museum
In Greenwich and far across the Atlantic where the Old World
    could not imagine 'em.

As the funeral boat makes its way slowly inland, down to Putney
    Bridge
In the direction of scenic Wimbledon Common, a swarm of red
    balloons are let fly,
One for every year of his young life, high up into a sunshine sky
And over a low-lying hovering ridge
Of cloud, that is competing with the sun
That has this unwelcome cloud on the run.

But one of the balloons has suddenly broken away from its
    tether too soon, ahead
Of the others, and in response to this, the youngest of the three
    children has said:

'Who's stolen this balloon, is it you dad who has taken the
    balloon? You bad dad.
I think I'll get my gun and shoot you dead.' So said this startled
    and confused little lad.

Disembarking at Putney Bridge the mourners – many of whom
    are from Hong Kong –
Are taking taxis and buses to Wimbledon Common for a meal in
    the favourite pub
Of bad dad, who regularly drank there before he listened to that
    centuries-old song
Of the inevitable and enticing sea
From the far end of the Thames Estuary.

Although he went to Hong Kong, appropriately enough by air,
It was the sea that took his mind and his heart there.

*Bob Crew*

## A FINAL THOUGHT

The redundant sea looks up at the sky
And wonders why
It got left behind
By the aeroplane
In the fast lane,
For which we can find
No body of poetry worthy of the name,
Because high-speed flights of shallow fancy are not at all the same
As deep oceans of highly stimulating seafaring. The name of the
      game
Has changed in favour of those tidal waves over head
That have not been romanced and imaginatively read
In the same way as the thought-provoking sea
That has swamped us with so much history and poetry.
It remains to be seen if airships will trigger, in the slow fullness
      of time,
As many narratives as we have about ships at sea, smothered in
      brine.
I suspect not. But is this the miserable failure of modern poetry,
Or is it that air travel cannot hold an inspirational candle to
      ships at sea?
Because the sea is all around us, on our doorstep, lapping our
      shores,
We do not feel estranged or alienated from it. But those distant
      heavens
Are set apart, somewhere else beyond the clouds, as we hurtle
      through them
In an enclosed, cramped and sealed-off space, firmly locked up
      indoors,
And hopefully out of harm's way. We are completely at sixes and
      sevens
With the outside world, as we spy on it through a tiny window
      when
Occasionally there is something to see. But we cannot take the
      heavens air,

As we take the sea air, and there are no decks from which to look
      out
And be exposed to the oceans of the world. There are no shores
      for us to
Stroll along when we reach for the skies. We really are out of it
      up there
In the sky, whereas at sea we are in the thick of it, which is why
      the last shout
Of poetry and literature will be echoed by intrepid seafarers as
      they come through,
Time and again, at one with nature, at one with themselves.
      They and the dramatic sea
Appeal to the imagination much more than aircraft overhead,
      and it will always be
So in a world globed in blue
And Emerson's drop of dew.

*Bob Crew*

# Bob Crew

Sixty-five-year-old Bob Crew lives in North London. He read English Literature at the University of London and is a poet and author of two other books currently in the bookstalls – *Gurkhas At War* and *The Beheading and Other True Stories* – as well as a forthcoming book of poetry, *The World's Husbands*.

He says that he should perhaps confess, in a book of this kind, that he has never seriously been to sea, other than in a troop ship from Cyprus to Southampton when he was a soldier in 1961, on crossings of the English Channel, and as a passenger on the QE2 when he took a cruise from Southampton to New York – and when mucking about on Chinese junks in the South China Seas.

But he has spent many happy hours rowing on the River Thames. He was born in Reading in Berkshire, and his grandfather, John Henry Cole, was a boat builder in the beautiful riverside village of Sonning. Bob Crew's late mother, Ivy Cole, only ever went to sea once, on a day trip with her husband across the English Channel to France.

Bob Crew would also like to point out that, notwithstanding the poetry that he and other poets have written about the French at the Battle of Trafalgar – capturing the triumphant mood of the times and commenting on the history of the period – he is a great admirer of Napoleon and of Republican France. He has travelled extensively in France and enjoyed the people, culture, art galleries and museums, the countryside and, most of all, the food. As far as he can tell, the surname Crew is Crue in French, and it is likely that his ancestors came to England with William the Conqueror from Normandy – where the so-called French were of Danish-Viking stock – later to depart to Ireland and become Carews, before returning to England as Crews.

Just to confuse the issue, there is a desert in South Africa called the Karoo Desert, and Bob Crew has crossed that ocean of sand on the famous Blue Train from Cape Town to Pretoria.

# Acknowledgements

The editor and publisher wish to thank the following for permission to use copyright material:

- The Society of Authors, as the Literary Representatives of the Estate of John Masefield, for 'Sea-fever', 'Cargoes', 'Trade winds', 'The west wind', 'The emigrant', 'To the seamen', and 'Thoughts for later on', by **John Masefield**. From *The Nine Days Wonder*, William Heinemann, 1941; and *The Oxford Library of English Poetry*, Vol. 3, Oxford University Press, 1987.

- Carcanet Press Ltd, for 'He was a thorn in our flesh', by **Robert Graves**. From *Complete Poems*, ed. B. Graves and D. Ward. Carcanet Press, 2000.

- Peter Newbolt, for 'Admirals all', by **Henry Newbolt**. From *Nelson: a Dream of Glory*, Jonathan Cape, 2004.

- The Society of Authors, as the Literary Representatives of the Estate of **Alfred Noyes**, for 'The phantom fleet', and 'Drake', by Alfred Noyes. From *Drake*, William Blackwood, 1908.

- A. P. Watt Ltd, on behalf of The National Trust for Places of Historic Interest or Natural Beauty, for 'A song in storm' by **Rudyard Kipling**. From *Poems*, Everyman's Library, 2001.

- Alan Holden, for 'Seaman 1941', by **Molly Holden**; © Alan Holden 2005. From *The Faber Book of 20th Century Women's Poetry*, Faber & Faber, 1987.

Every effort has been made to trace the copyright holders of the poems published in this book. The editor and publisher apologise if any material has been included without permission or without appropriate acknowledgement, and would be glad to be told of anyone who has not been consulted.